D1020580

DATE DUE

OCT 25 2000			
GAYLORD			PRINTED IN U.S.A.

3 1215 00059 4413

PHOTOGRAPHING THE FRONTIER

PHOTOGRAPHING THE FRONTIER

Dorothy and Thomas Hoobler

G. P. Putnam's Sons
New York

(title page photograph)
WILLIAM H. JACKSON: Mammoth Hot Springs in Yellowstone Valley. This was one of the photographs taken in 1871 that was included in the portfolio of prints Hayden presented to the members of Congress, prompting them to make Yellowstone the first national park. U.S. Geological Survey

Library of Congress Cataloging in Publication Data
Hoobler, Dorothy.
Photographing the frontier.
Bibliography: p.
Includes index.
SUMMARY: Discusses early photographic images of the
West and the photographers responsible for these
photographic records.
1. Photography—The West—History—Juvenile litera-
ture. 2. Photographers—The West—Biography—Juvenile
literature. [1. Photography—History. 2. Photogra-
phers. 3. The West—Social life and customs]
I. Hoobler, Thomas, joint author. II. Title.
TR23.6.H66 1979   770′.92′2 [B]   79-11130
ISBN 0-399-20694-9

CONTENTS

PHOTOGRAPHING ❦ THE FRONTIER ❦

1
EARLY PHOTOGRAPHERS OF THE WEST

In 1839, the American frontier began approximately at the Mississippi River. Except in the south, where Louisiana, Missouri, and Arkansas were already states, the land beyond the Mississippi contained only a few white settlers. California, the Southwest, and Texas were still Mexican territory. The settlements in the Pacific Northwest were reachable by a long ocean voyage. Only the hardiest of explorers had journeyed overland from the Mississippi to the Pacific.

Yet in the half century that followed, this vast land area would be crossed and settled by miners, homesteaders, railroad builders, and ranchers. In 1890, the superintendent of the census announced there no longer was a frontier. This period of expansion, exploration, and settlement would become famous in legend and history as the era of the Wild West. Contributing to its development, recording and publicizing the taming of the frontier, were the cameramen. For the first time in history, later ages could look back and say, "This was the way it really looked. This was the way the West was settled."

For the year 1839 also marked the announcement of an amazing discovery. The Frenchman Louis Daguerre and his partner Nicephore Niepce had devised a way to make permanent images from life on shiny, mirror-like plates, using only the light from the sun and chemicals. A moment in history could be permanently recorded, accurate in every detail.

Daguerreotyping, as the new invention became known, caught the imagination of the world. Crowds lined up wherever one of the shiny, mirror-like images was displayed. The appeal of the daguerreotypes—to an age which had never seen an image, as we have, reproduced by the millions in magazines, motion pictures, and television—was in their perfect rendering of reality. One writer expressed the awe felt toward daguerreotyping by calling it "the pencil of nature."

Paintings of historical events and places could give a general idea of what they looked like, but the view was filtered through the talent and style of an artist. A painting was limited to one person's impression of what something looked like. The daguerreotype showed a slice of reality. Photography was a way of extending the vision of humanity. A daguerreotype made of a distant place could be transported across continents and oceans—as many soon were—to show the actuality of famous people and places.

In the West, the daguerreotype and later photographic developments would show the cowboys, the Indians, the soldiers, the railroads, developing towns, the exploring expeditions, and the faces of hundreds of thousands of travelers who went west.

In an age of slow transportation and communications, photography was a means of staying close to loved ones thousands of miles away. As the covered wagons rolled west, most people brought daguerreotypes of loved ones as a link with home. Those who journeyed west sent their own pictures home; often the changes were astonishing to their families. A man in Havana, New York, wrote of his son: "We received Ronald's ambrotype [a later type of photograph], and had his name not been inside, we would not have known it. When he left home he was a smooth-faced, good-looking boy, and he sends home the likeness of an ourangoutang with the upper part of his face shaved!"

Photography was also a public link between the "States," as westerners called the East, and the frontier. Photographs showed the West as it really was, not as the myth that had been characterized both as the "Garden of the World" and "The Great American Desert." Lithographs made from photographic images were reproduced in newspapers, magazines, and books, igniting the imagination and ambition of men and women who would seek their fortunes in the new region. The value of the photograph as publicity soon became apparent. Pictures of incredible, previously unknown scenery helped to promote settlement and governmental protection of certain areas as national parks.

Thousands of photographs of the West are preserved in archives today. Many are uncredited, for most of the photographers are not known. The surviving photographs represent only a fraction of those that were made. Fire caused the destruction of many. Also, most daguerreotypists didn't copy the pictures they took and the pictures scattered with the customers who bought them and were lost in succeeding generations.

Photographers in the West were often isolated. They lacked adequate equipment, information on technical advances in the trade, or the advice and company of fellow photographers. Photography was not an easy business, nor usually a lucrative one. Often photography was only a sideline, practiced by self-taught individuals or those who had a short apprenticeship in an established gallery.

The life of a photographer was hard and often unrewarding. More than a few careers ended in alcoholism, madness, or suicide. Photographers, as residents of the frontier, were sometimes participants in events, sometimes observers there to capture the moment, and they sometimes left only a picture. In countless cases, not even the photographer's name has survived. This book presents only a few of the intrepid men and women who left us an invaluable record of one of the most colorful periods of our country's past.

Among the earliest Americans to take up daguerreotyping as a business was John Plumbe, Jr. Plumbe's tragic life was bound up with the early history of photography and the West. Born in Great Britain, he came to the United States at the age of twelve, worked as a railroad surveyor, and became a lawyer in what was then the frontier town of Dubuque, Iowa. Plumbe's experience in the West convinced him of the feasibility of a transcontinental railroad. He came to Washington, D.C., in 1840 to find support in Congress for his idea, with no success.

While in Washington, however, Plumbe became interested in daguerreotyping. He became one of the earliest professional daguerreotypists, and by 1845 he was operating a chain of galleries, or depots, as he called them. Many early daguerreotypists first learned their trade in one of Plumbe's galleries. Their names appear among those who later went to California to establish their own galleries during the gold rush boom.

Plumbe had galleries in most major eastern cities, as well as Dubuque, St. Louis, and Harrodsburgh Springs, Kentucky. The western galleries doubtless photographed pioneers heading west, and may have contributed to the exhibition of Plumbe's pictures that was displayed at the National Fair at Washington in May, 1846. Unfortunately, only a few of the thousands of daguerreotypes Plumbe's galleries produced have ever been discovered.

Plumbe spent the profits from his galleries in financing his railroad scheme. In 1847, the galleries ran into financial difficulty, and Plumbe had to declare bankruptcy. Two years later, he followed the scramble of pioneers seeking gold in California, but like the majority of them he went bust. (The gold, had he known it, was in his pictures. Several of Plumbe's daguerreotypes were discovered in a California flea market in 1972. A single one of them was sold to a collector for $14,000.)

Plumbe returned to Dubuque a broken man. His idea for a transcontinental railroad, too early for its time, had been ridiculed as being as silly as building "a railroad to the moon." He committed suicide in 1857.

Besides pictures of settlers headed west, gallery operators in the towns on the edge of the frontier also took the earliest photographs of Indians. J. H. Fitzgibbon of St. Louis showed portraits of "Indian warriors" at the New York Crystal Palace exhibition of 1853. In 1858, it was reported that he "twice visited the Indian Nations, bringing back each time an admirable collection of Indian portraits."

Fitzgibbon began his career as a daguerreotypist in Lynchburg, Virginia, in 1841, and was operating a gallery in St. Louis by 1847. Two years later, his success had bought him a sixteen-room gallery doing a lively business. Fitzgibbon operated a high-class establishment, cautioning those seeking "cheap" views that a daguerreotype by Fitzgibbon cost no less than $3 nor more than $40. This compared with prices in a "cheap" gallery that might be as low as 25¢.

Unfortunately, most of Fitzgibbon's work is lost to us today. He sold his gallery, along with his collection of daguerreotypes, five years before his death in 1882. If found, his pictures would be as valuable as Plumbe's.

Another daguerreotypist working in St. Louis was Thomas Easterly, who was born in Brattleboro, Vermont. In the early 1840s,

THOMAS EASTERLY: Chief Keokuk of the Sacs. Probably made in Iowa around 1847, when Easterly was an itinerant daguerreotypist. Keokuk was known as a friend of the whites, and kept his tribe peaceful during the Black Hawk War. St. Louis Historical Society

he worked as an itinerant daguerreotypist, hauling his equipment in a wagon that served as both darkroom and studio. There were many such itinerant photographers in the early years, visiting places that were too small to have a resident daguerreotypist. Some even outfitted houseboats as floating galleries, stopping at towns along the rivers. For those who were learning the trade, it was good experience.

In 1848, Easterly found permanent employment in a gallery in St. Louis. He soon took over the business from the former owner. As was the custom of gallery proprietors of the time, he displayed sample daguerreotypes on his wall as an attraction to draw potential customers. He advertised "likenesses of Distinguished Statesmen, Eminent Divines, Prominent Citizens, Indian Chiefs, and Notorious Robbers and Murderers. Also—Beautiful Landscapes, Perfect Clouds, and a Bona Fide Streak of Lightning, Taken on the Night of June 18th, 1847." Easterly took a daguerreotype of Chief Keokuk of the Sacs in 1847 that is probably the earliest Indian photograph still in existence.

Easterly failed to take advantage of the technical advances in photography that made the daguerreotype process outmoded. In 1866, Easterly was the only photographer still exhibiting daguer-reotypes at the national photographer's convention. By that time, his studio's business had so declined that he was operating from his home.

Gradually, Easterly was forced to sell his collection of daguer-reotypes to others. Fitzgibbon bought some of them and sold numerous copies—made by the new "wet-plate" process—under his own name. This was a common practice among photographers of the day. Sometimes they didn't even pay a courtesy fee, but pirated outright the photographs of others. This practice makes it difficult today to accurately identify the person who took many of the photographs that survive.

When Easterly died in 1882, his daguerreotypes were gone, his business was defunct, and he was all but forgotten.

After 1850, the "wet-plate" process became the usual method by which photographs were taken. Between then and 1880—the chief period covered in the later chapters of this book—virtually every photographer of the West made pictures by the wet-plate process.

16

In the wet-plate method, a clear sheet of glass was coated with a thick solution of collodion that was sensitive to light. The coated plate could be used in a camera and developed as long as it remained wet. The result was a photographic negative that could be used to make any number of prints. One drawback of the daguerreotype had been that the mercury-coated plate used in the camera produced a positive image that could only be reproduced by making another daguerreotype of it. Any number of prints could be made from a developed collodion negative plate, giving the photographers a new source of income through the sale of prints of a famous person or place.

The wet-plate process also made possible the mass production of stereo cards, which were made in the millions during the decades between 1850 and 1900 and were a major source of income for many photographers. A stereo card was a piece of stiff cardboard (early ones were also made on glass or tissue) commonly measuring about 7" wide by 3½" high. On the card were two photographs about 3" × 3". When viewed through a stereoscopic viewer, the images merged to become a three-dimensional view. In the late nineteenth century, the stereoscope was as common in middle-class American homes as the television set is today. Both as an educational tool and as entertainment, the stereoscope significantly influenced American life. For the first time, masses of people could see distant places, prominent people, and have a permanent visual record of historical events—all in three dimensions and in the comfort of the family parlor.

Among the most popular subjects for stereo cards were the scenery, settlements, Indians, and soldiers of the West. From the beginning, the West had an appeal for the armchair traveler seeking vicarious entertainment. Railroads and land developers used the cards as a means of publicity to attract travelers and settlers. Virtually none of the photographers of the West ventured forth without bringing along a twin-lensed camera that was capable of making plates for stereo views. Thousands of these cards can still be found in flea markets and antique shops today. Each one was made from an individual pair of prints, usually hand-made by the photographer or a darkroom assistant.

The chief drawback of the wet-plate process, for a photographer

17

traveling the frontier, was that the plates had to be made and developed within half an hour or less. This meant that a photographer had to take with him the equivalent of a fully-stocked photographic darkroom, which could weigh hundreds of pounds. For washing the developed plate, a source of fresh water was necessary. The photographer who traveled with an expedition could not afford to hold up the group's progress. The time it required to coat a plate (inside some kind of portable darkroom), make the picture, and then return to the darkroom to develop the plate, and finally to wash it, often meant the photographer had to travel far ahead or behind the group he was with. Being alone on the frontier was often a dangerous business.

In the 1840's pioneers began to travel along the Oregon Trail in increasing numbers. The trail began at Independence or St. Joseph, Missouri, moved westward along the Platte River, through the South Pass in the Central Rockies and northwest to the Columbia River, along which lay the early settlements in the Oregon Territory. Among the first photographers to bring his equipment across the continent on this route was Peter Britt.

Britt was a portrait painter who emigrated from Switzerland as a young man. He learned daguerreotyping from Fitzgibbon of St. Louis in 1847. Britt then operated his own gallery in Highland, Illinois, until 1852, when he struck out with three friends bound for Portland, Oregon.

The four travelers brought with them a wagon containing their supplies and Britt's 300 pounds of daguerreotype equipment. The trip to Ft. Laramie, Wyoming, 600 miles from St. Joseph, was uneventful but grueling. After leaving Ft. Laramie, however, Britt's party encountered a band of Sioux Indians, who surrounded their wagon, bringing it to a stop. Britt's friends were ready to open fire, but Britt persuaded them to hold off. Some of the Indians rode up to the wagon and spread a blanket. Britt threw in some food, the blanket was gathered up, and the Indians rode off.

Crossing the Rockies was the most dangerous part of the Oregon trip. The travelers passed the bones of animals and the graves of those who had come to grief before. An argument over the best path to follow beyond the South Pass led the party to divide their supplies. They even sawed the wagon in half—each group of two got a two-wheeled cart to continue its separate way. All eventually arrived safely in Portland after an eight-month journey.

Portland did not appeal to Britt. Rumors of the gold strikes in the southern part of the state caused him to move to the Rogue River Valley, where a town named Jacksonville was springing from the wilderness.

Britt made a claim in the mining area and worked for several weeks, finding in all 75¢ worth of gold. Sensibly deciding to work at what he knew best, he opened a daguerrian studio in Jacksonville. For the next half century, Britt would photograph the life and people of a frontier town growing into a modern city, as well as the scenery of southern Oregon. He became a local legend and the leading citizen of Jacksonville. Photographs of his later career—described in Chapter Five—are numerous, but if he took any of that early wagon train, they do not survive.

Photographing the Northwest at the same time, but from the viewpoint of a career army officer, was Lorenzo Lorain. Born in Pennsylvania in 1831, Lorain entered West Point in 1852. On receiving his commission, he was assigned to Ft. Walla Walla in Washington Territory. The army there was engaged in a struggle with the local Indians in what became known as the Yakima War.

In a pattern that would become familiar throughout the West, mining strikes in the area had brought thousands of white miners to a territory which the U.S. Government had assigned by treaty to the Indians. Armed skirmishes followed, and the army was assigned to protect the settlers and pacify the Indians through force. Lorain's diary shows how little he liked the task, and that he felt a great deal of sympathy for the Indians in contrast to the "parcel of white animals calling themselves men, and for whose protection the army is kept in most disagreeable situations in advance of civilization."

The earliest Lorain photographs that survive were taken during his tour of duty at Ft. Walla Walla. These are views of The Dalles, a town on the Columbia River near which the Indians had killed fifteen people working at a river crossing. Lorain called The Dalles, "the meanest place I ever saw."

In late 1857, Lorain went to Ft. Umpqua, in southwest Oregon, to serve with the garrison guarding a nearby Indian reservation. While at Ft. Umpqua he met Dr. E. P. Vollum, another enthusiastic

19

amateur photographer, and the two men, using wet plates, photographed life at the fort and among the settlers in the Lower Umpqua River valley.

In 1859, trouble began between the ranchers of the Rogue River valley and the Klamath Indians. A detachment of men, including Lorain, went to Jacksonville in 1860 to restore order. Lorain managed to take his cumbersome camera equipment with him, and took some views of the troops in the area. There is no record of his having met Peter Britt, but Britt's gallery was a logical place for Lorain to obtain supplies. In any case, Lorain's opinion of Jacksonville was unfavorable. He wrote, "I have never seen a place in which the people appeared more anxious to 'make money' or seemed to have less."

LORENZO LORAIN: Company "L" of the 3rd Artillery, at Camp Day, Oregon, 1857 or 1858. The temporary camp was probably a stopping-place for Lorain's troops while away from Ft. Umpqua. Oregon Historical Society

Lorain was called east for service in the Civil War. He was disabled at the First Battle of Manassas, and continued his army career as an instructor. His interest in photography led him to establish a photographic department at Ft. Monroe Artillery School in the seventies. His later photographs were lost after his death in 1882. The early views of the Washington and Oregon Territories, some in an album owned by his family, others in the possession of the heirs of Dr. Vollum, lay undiscovered until the 1940s.

One group of determined pioneers went west seeking religious freedom. The members of the Church of Latter-Day Saints, founded by Joseph Smith in 1830, had sought a place where they could practice their religion almost from its beginning. Several hundred

21

Church members, commonly known as the Mormons, had followed Smith from New York State to Missouri and then to Nauvoo, Illinois. A daguerreotypist named Lucian R. Foster, from New York City, established a gallery in Nauvoo in 1844. Foster probably made the only daguerreotype of Smith before the Mormon leader's death at the hands of a lynch mob in June, 1844. Foster himself was a devout Mormon and was president of the New York branch of the Church in 1841. But he was "cut off" from the Church in a doctrinal dispute, and remained behind when the Mormons emigrated to Utah.

The great Mormon trek across the Plains under the leadership of Brigham Young took place in 1846. Young led his flock to the Great Salt Lake, where they built their city. No pictures of the epic migration are known.

Soon, there were daguerreotypists in Salt Lake City to record its early days. One of the first was Marsena Cannon. He had been born in 1812 in New Hampshire and worked in Plumbe's Boston gallery in the late 1840s, around the time Cannon converted to Mormonism. For a few years after the Plumbe chain dissolved, Cannon and William Shew continued to operate the gallery in Boston. In 1850, Cannon and his family left for Utah.

Cannon's early photographs show the groundbreaking of the Salt Lake Temple in 1853, along with many of the other early buildings of the city. The earliest known daguerreotype of Brigham Young was taken by Cannon in 1855.

Cannon advertised frequently in the *Deseret News*, the local newspaper, on occasion declaring his willingness to exchange "hay, oats, peas, beans, butter, eggs, fox and wolf skins and cash for Likenesses." A drawing of a large cannon always appeared in the ads, and the "sign of the cannon" marked the location of his shop as well.

In 1861, Cannon was selected to go with a group of Mormons to southern Utah to settle one of the growing number of Mormon communities in the area. If the assignment meant the end of his daguerreotype business, it was a sacrifice he was willing to make for his Church. Cannon turned the gallery over to a young assistant named Charles R. Savage, who would later become one of the most famous photographers of the West.

22

Cannon did not return to Salt Lake City until 1869. He did not resume his business, and left the Church and the city five years later. He died in San Francisco, sometime after 1899.

The cession of New Mexico and California to the United States in 1848 opened up new areas of the frontier. In 1848, gold was discovered at Sutter's Mill, near present-day Sacramento, California. The discovery touched off the greatest influx of would-be millionaires the West has ever seen. From all over the "States" and the world people came, attracted by tales of instant wealth. Those leaving home often outfitted themselves in prospector's gear and had their daguerreotypes taken. The surge in daguerreotype business created a competitive situation that resulted in the rise of the "cheap" galleries. Daguerreotypists were among those heading west, some to seek gold, and others to find a thriving business in the burgeoning city of San Francisco.

San Francisco was the jumping-off place for the gold fields. Ships lay deserted in the harbor where their crews had jumped ship to join the hunt for gold. In 1848, the city was a tiny settlement of fewer than a thousand people. Seven years later, it boasted a thriving commerce and a population of 55,000. In 1850 the first daguerreotypist appeared in the San Francisco city directory: Mrs. Julia Shannon, whose other specialty was midwifery.

The demand back East for photographs of the gold fields and the frontier led to one of the most ambitious photographic expeditions ever. John Wesley Jones toured the United States in the 1850s exhibiting his "Pantoscope of California." A pantoscope was a huge painting or series of paintings that was accompanied by a lecturer explaining the various scenes. It was a popular entertainment.

Jones claimed his pantoscope was based on 1,500 daguerreotypes he had taken on a journey from the Pacific Ocean to the Mississippi River around 1851. The daguerreotypes and the pantoscope itself are lost to history, but newspaper records show that Jones advertised for photographers to contribute to his collection.

The story of Jones's epic journey is told in a book that Jones commissioned. Written in a dramatic and flowery style, it may be a mixture of tall tale and fact, although drawings made of Jones's daguerreotypes exist to corroborate part of the story. Jones was accompanied by three other daguerreotypists, William and Jacob Shew, and S. L. Shaw.

A typical episode on the trip occurred near a rock formation known as Steeple Rocks in what is today Idaho. There, the Jones party was ambushed by Indians. Several members, including Jones, were wounded, but Jones insisted on persevering in the attempt to photograph the rocks. The account continues:

> But Indians were lurking behind every rock, and dangers stood thick around. The company were not for stopping . . . Fired with the excitement of the moment, our Artist forgot his wounds and debility, and rising from his litter said, "Gentlemen, I shall daguerreotype this scenery though deserted by every man. Who will volunteer to stay with me?" . . . His faithful men gathered around him and the work commenced. Sick and faint the artist directed and accomplished the task.

Robert H. Vance, one of the most successful of the early California photographers, exhibited 300 large daguerreotypes in New York in 1851. Vance's exhibit included many views of the gold miners at work; San Francisco and surrounding communities; Sutter's Mill; and many of the Indian tribes inhabiting the Pacific Coast.

Vance had spent more than $3,000 collecting and making his daguerreotype collection, and it was enthusiastically praised by eastern critics. He tried to sell the collection at a profit and failed, finally disposing of it to Jeremiah Gurney, a New York daguerreotypist, for $1,500. Gurney resold the daguerreotypes to Fitzgibbon of St. Louis, but what became of them after that is unknown.

Vance returned to California and eventually established a chain of daguerrian galleries in San Francisco and other cities. Men who learned their trade in these galleries took many of the important photographs of the California frontier.

The operator of Vance's San Jose gallery suddenly quit his job and Vance had to send an untrained young man named Carleton E. Watkins to keep the gallery in order for a few days. Vance gave Watkins a little instruction in how to prepare a daguerreotype plate, and said that he should tell anyone whose portrait he took to come back for it in a week. By that time, Vance would have come down to retake the daguerreotypes. But when Vance arrived, he found that

24

Watkins was turning out acceptable work, and left him in charge. It was the beginning of one of the great photographic careers of the West.

In the 1850s Vance adopted the wet-plate process and returned to the gold diggings to make another set of photographs of the miners at work. He took with him a huge 11" × 14" view camera. The photographs, which still survive, give one of the few authentic portrayals of the gold rush.

For several years, Vance was well known as San Francisco's leading photographer. He sold his galleries in 1861, the San Francisco one going to another promising young assistant, Charles L. Weed. Vance returned to New York, where he died in 1876.

William Shew, who ran Plumbe's gallery in Boston with Marsena Cannon, was attracted by the tales of the fabulous riches awaiting in California. He shipped an entire wagon containing a fully-equipped darkroom and studio by ship around Cape Horn to San Francisco. Though it must have been cumbersome, the portable studio proved useful in the notoriously fire-plagued city. On at least one occasion, Shew managed to hire a team of horses just in time to pull his studio away from a burning building. He set up business in a vacant lot, bringing down the ire of the authorities, who demanded that he move. It was about this time that he and his brother departed on the Jones expedition.

When the Shews returned to San Francisco, they rented permanent quarters for their new gallery. Sure enough, within a month they were wiped out by a fire. Undaunted, the Shews moved their gallery to fashionable Montgomery Street, where they began to attract a high-class business. William Shew continued his career for more than a half century. Fortunately for history, he recorded more than the faces of the wealthy and famous who visited his gallery. He roamed the Mexican section of town, making an invaluable record of life there.

The most comprehensive photographic record of early San Francisco is the *San Francisco Album,* a book containing thirty-three wet-plate prints, published in 1856. It is said to be the earliest book containing photographs of an American city. For each copy of the book, the thirty-three prints were individually made and glued in by hand. The photographer was G. R. Fardon, whose other activities in

WILLIAM SHEW: *A prospecting site near Placerville, California, in 1851.*
Bancroft Library

G. R. FARDON: View down Sacramento Street, San Francisco. In the center of the picture can be seen a sign marking the location of Vance's Daguerrean Rooms. Skylights on the roof let in the brilliant light necessary for taking daguerreotypes. Courtesy of the New-York Historical Society, New York City

San Francisco are unknown. He later worked his way up the coast to Victoria, British Columbia, where he took a number of stereo views of the Canadian West.

Stereo views of California were immediately popular, but photographers using the wet-plate process soon found that the western scenery demanded huge photographs. Since enlargements made from small plates were not practical at the time, the photographers brought with them huge cameras capable of making large glass negatives.

In June, 1859, C. L. Weed, Vance's assistant, made a historic trip to the Yosemite Valley, bringing both a stereo camera and a huge

28

box that made glass plates measuring about 10″ × 15″. Each plate alone weighed about one and a half pounds. Weed's photographs were used by a promoter of the Yosemite area, James Hutchings, to make lithographs to illustrate a series of articles that appeared in Hutchings's *California Magazine.* Vance's gallery also sold copies of the prints.

The Yosemite Valley was one of the first of the western scenes to capture the imagination of photographers. The cliffs covered with trees and unusual rock formations, the giant Sequoias that were taller than any previously known trees, and the breathtaking falls of the Yosemite—the second highest waterfall in the world—were a treasure trove for a photographer seeking to make a name as an artist.

Carleton Watkins, by now operating his own gallery in San Francisco, made another series of Yosemite views in 1861. He constructed his own camera specifically for the trip. It took a mammoth 18″ × 22″ plate. Watkins's equipment, including not only the customary stereo camera but the supplies for developing such huge plates in the field, required twelve mules to be transported. He had to travel over crude trails to get to the wild Yosemite country. Even after establishing camp, he took along five mules for each day's shooting.

Photographic materials of the time were "slow," requiring long exposure times. Watkins recalled having to make an hour-long exposure for an early morning view of the valley. It was necessary to photograph only when no wind was blowing, or the leaves and branches of the trees would be blurred. Watkins's views are razor-sharp and displayed in their full size are as majestic as any picture taken with modern equipment.

The Yosemite pictures gave Watkins a national reputation. They earned him the praise of the prestigious photographic journal *The Philadelphia Photographer* and the respect of other photographers throughout the country. In 1868, Watkins received a medal for his California views at a Paris exhibition.

Capitalizing on his fame, Watkins named his new gallery on Montgomery Street the Yosemite Art Gallery. He was able to market his stereo and large-plate pictures under his own name, a significant accomplishment. Large firms such as Lawrence and Houseworth in

San Francisco commonly bought the work of free-lance photographers for sale in their extensive stereo card lines. The Lawrence and Houseworth series is thought to include many of Weed's photographs, without credit to Weed.

In 1868, Watkins made his first trip to the Oregon country where he photographed the logging industry and some of the scenery and frontier communities. Each summer thereafter Watkins would pack his stereo camera and 18" x 22"-plate camera and travel through the Northwest, making new pictures for his stereo series. Watkins's wife kept the gallery operating to allow him time for these trips.

Watkins had a long career, and not always a happy one. The financial panic of 1872–73 resulted in his losing control of both his gallery and the fine collection of plates he had made. Another photographer began issuing Watkins's views under his own name. Watkins recovered, and began a second series of views, which he exhibited at the Centennial Fair of 1876.

Watkins's friendship with Collis Huntington, the railroad magnate, brought him further work, and a free railroad pass which he used to travel through the West making photographs. In 1906, the great San Francisco earthquake and the resulting fires wiped out Watkins's gallery once more. By this time, the old man was almost blind and unable to work, and he accepted relief from a fund set up by the American Photographers Society. His mind failed before his body, and he was confined in a mental hospital. Huntington arranged for his release, and he lived with his wife on a small ranch until his death in 1916.

One of the giants in the history of photography began his career in San Francisco shortly after the gold rush. Eadweard Muybridge is remembered today primarily for his later work with photographic studies of motion, which led to the development of motion pictures. But his landscape views of the West would be sufficient to make his career memorable.

Muybridge was born Edward Muggeridge in England in 1830. He

CARLETON E. WATKINS: The "Grizzly Giant," one of the famous Sequoia trees in a grove near Yosemite Valley. Rare Book Division, New York Public Library, Astor, Lenox and Tilden Foundations

changed his name to fit the spelling of the name of a Saxon king. By 1850, he was in New York, where he learned daguerreotyping from Silas Selleck. Muybridge arrived in San Francisco around 1855, when the city was a battleground between ex-prospectors who had turned to crime and a local vigilante committee. In this environment, the optimistic Muybridge opened a bookstore, where he also

CARLETON E. WATKINS: The Albion lumber mill, 115 miles north of San Francisco, photographed in the late 1860s. The cloud of steam on the left of the photograph is from a water-cooled high-speed saw. Chutes to bring the felled trees down from the hills above can be seen on both the left and right. The Bancroft Library

sold photographic copies of fine paintings. He made the acquaintance of a number of local photographers, and may have worked with Weed on the Yosemite trip.

Muybridge had the idea of distributing the work of California photographers in England. On an overland trip to the East, he made a detour to Texas, where the stagecoach overturned, severely injuring him. He recuperated for some years in Europe, where he worked on inventions—a washing machine for clothes and an apparatus for printing photographs.

Muybridge reappeared in San Francisco in 1867. His friend Selleck was now operating a photographic gallery there, and Muybridge began taking pictures and marketing them through Selleck's gallery. He outfitted a horse-drawn wagon to carry his photographic equipment, and painted on it the slogan, "Helios—the Flying Studio." Helios became Muybridge's trademark.

From the first, Muybridge was an energetic and far-traveling photographer. In 1868, he spent six months photographing Yosemite, a daring venture in view of the popularity of others' work there. But Muybridge's photographs were judged superior even to Watkins's, and he was a skilled enough publicist to capitalize on his efforts. He prepared presentation sets of the photos for the Mercantile Library of San Francisco, and sent 125 prints to *The Philadelphia Photographer*, which praised them in extravagant terms. Muybridge had to obtain an eastern agent to handle sales of his prints in the "States."

The next year, Muybridge accompanied an expedition to the newly purchased territory of Alaska. His photographs of the trip were widely circulated and gave Americans an awareness of the potential of the new territory. He continued to do work for government agencies after returning to San Francisco, photographing sites for lighthouses and navigation signals along the Pacific Coast.

On some of these trips, Muybridge collaborated with Albert Bierstadt, who was working on some of the great paintings of western scenery that later brought him fame. Muybridge was fascinated by Bierstadt's rendering of the vast, cloud-filled skies that are a characteristic of his paintings. Photographic materials at the time did not have a great enough latitude to record both landscape

EADWEARD MUYBRIDGE: Falls of the Yosemite from Glacier Rock. The falls, second highest in the world, were a favorite for Yosemite photographers, but the angle and the figure perched on a rock were touches that distinguished Muybridge's work from others. University of California Library

and cloud effects, and in most photographs the sky was a blank.

Muybridge adjusted his chemicals and exposure times so that he could photograph the sky by itself to show cloud formations. He superimposed these negatives on ordinary ones of scenery to produce pictures that recorded the full range of nature. He used this technique in taking a second series of Yosemite pictures in 1872. The photographs were exhibited as far away as Vienna and Berlin, where residents viewed them with the awe we reserve today for pictures from another planet.

Muybridge's career was interrupted by his trial for the murder of his wife's lover. Insanity was the defense offered by Muybridge's lawyer. His agent, William Rulofson, testified that Muybridge was careless with money, had photographed himself precariously perched on the edge of a 3,400-foot cliff above the Yosemite Valley, and that he refused to take a picture that offended his artistic taste no matter how much money was offered. As further proof of insanity, Silas Selleck recalled that when Muybridge returned from Europe with new photographic supplies, he refused to sell them to Selleck but told him to use them as if they were his own. The jury, impressed by such testimony, returned a verdict of not guilty.

Muybridge made a photographic trip to Central America during the next two years, but in 1876 he returned to San Francisco. He set to work making a 360-degree panoramic picture of the city in eleven sections, measuring seven and a half feet in length. Three decades earlier San Francisco had been a tent village of muddy paths and Spanish pueblos. Now, Muybridge's camera surveyed a great city. Banks, schools, the Custom House, the headquarters of the Central Pacific Railroad, the U.S. Mint, the stock exchange, insurance companies, theaters, and grand hotels had taken the place of the rugged little village. The frontier had come and gone from San Francisco in less than thirty years, a progression that had been well documented by the city's photographers.

California's wealth had been the attraction for thousands of settlers who came west across the Plains in the meantime. A great continental railroad had been built to tie the West Coast to the East. But before any of this, back once more in 1840, surveyors and explorers had set out on the task of mapping the West. Congress had sponsored many expeditions to complete this work, and on some of them, cumbersome daguerreotype equipment was taken along to record the terrain.

The first expedition across the Mississippi on which an attempt was made to take daguerreotypes was led by John C. Fremont in 1842. On the first of his five major expeditions through the West, Fremont explored the Platte River through the South Pass of the Rockies. Fremont attempted to make the daguerreotypes himself, to the wry amusement of another member of the group, Charles Preuss, a German. Preuss wrote in his diary:

Yesterday afternoon and this morning Fremont set up his daguerreotype to photograph the rocks; he spoiled five plates that way. Not a thing was to be seen on them. That's the way it often is with these Americans. They know everything, they can do everything, and when they are put to the test, they fail miserably. . . . Today he said the air up here is too thin; that is the reason his daguerreotype was a failure. Old boy, you don't understand the thing, that is it.

On a later expedition, Fremont engaged the services of a professional daguerreotypist, Solomon Nunez Carvalho, who was more successful. This was in 1853, when the wet-plate process was beginning to replace the daguerreotype. Fremont held a short "contest" between Carvalho and a wet-plate photographer named Bomar to determine which man would go on the trip. As Bomar was unable to produce pictures without letting the finished plates wash in water overnight, and Carvalho could turn out a satisfactory daguerreotype in half an hour, Fremont chose Carvalho.

The expedition left Westport, Kansas, in late September, 1853, with twenty-two men including ten Delaware chiefs as guides. It was to travel along the 38th parallel to find the most desirable railway route to the Pacific. Carvalho, then thirty-eight years old, was also a talented painter, but he is best known today for his detailed account of the journey. Fremont's notes on the expedition were lost in a fire.

Professional friends doubted that Carvalho could take photographs under the harsh weather conditions that the expedition would encounter. Crossing mountains in temperatures that could drop as low as 30° below zero would make daguerreotyping impossible. A necessary stage of the daguerreotype process was to expose the metal plate to iodine fumes, which ordinarily required a temperature above 70°F. Carvalho managed to make daguerreotypes in spite of this, but just how he did it will always remain a mystery. He wrote later: "I shall not appear egotistical if I say that I encountered many difficulties, but I was well prepared to meet them by having previously acquired a scientific and practical knowledge of the chemicals I used, as well as of the theory of light: a firm determination to succeed also aided me."

Along the way, Fremont's party encountered a Cheyenne village. Carvalho left the first account of the Indians' reaction to seeing their own photographs. "I had great difficulty in getting them to sit still (so the picture would not be blurred) or even to submit to have themselves daguerreotyped. I made a picture, first, of their lodges, which I showed them. I then made one of the old woman and papoose. When they saw it, they thought I was a 'supernatural being'; and, before I left camp, they were satisfied I was more than human."

The party ran into difficulties when Fremont fell ill and had to return to St. Louis. While waiting for his return, Carvalho used the time to photograph the surrounding area. He tried to photograph buffalo herds nearby, but their constant movement spoiled his pictures, although he did take some shots of distant herds. A prairie fire was another subject that proved resistant to daguerreotyping. When Fremont returned, the party pushed on, but a band of Indians stole some of their horses and supplies.

As the group made their way into the foothills of the Rocky Mountains, the nights became colder, and the travelers often slept on the snow-covered ground. They had Indian rubber blankets to lie on, and wrapped themselves in buffalo robes. Carvalho recorded being awakened by one of the Indians in the middle of the night to take his turn at watching the horses. For two hours he walked around the band of horses in several feet of snow, stamping his feet to keep the circulation going. When he returned to camp, he cut a piece of liver from a frozen horse they had bought from the Indians for food and ate it raw. All around him his companions were covered with freshly fallen snow in what looked to Carvalho like "living graves."

Starvation and cold began to take their toll on the group. Sick men were left at the few settlements the party encountered. Carvalho himself lost 44 pounds (from his original 145) on the trip. At one point, the company made a solemn promise that whatever happened they would not resort to cannibalism. Butchering the mules and horses for food, they began to leave more of the other supplies behind them. Finally the daguerreotype apparatus was discarded in the snow.

The emaciated and sick Carvalho was left in a Mormon settlement where he was nursed back to health. Fremont took the daguerreotype plates on to California. He sent them to the studio of the New York photographer Mathew Brady to be copied. Fremont gave the original plates to a lithographer to illustrate the final report of the expedition, which unfortunately was never finished because Fremont turned his energies to running unsuccessfully for President.

Fremont's wife, who wrote that "almost all the plates were beautifully clear," recalled that the plates were lost in the same fire that destroyed Fremont's notes from the journey. The copies that Brady made have never been found, and one of the earliest records of the West was lost, like so much of the early daguerreotypists' work. Carvalho lived on till 1897.

Other surveys of the early West are known to have employed photographers, but little record of their work remains other than a few references in diaries or reports. Like Carvalho, many of those early survey photographers were also painters. J. M. Stanley first visited the West in 1843, when he made a number of paintings of Indians. In 1853, Stanley brought photographic equipment with him on the expedition led by Governor I. I. Stevens of Washington Territory to survey a northern route for the transcontinental railroad. At Ft. Benton, Stevens wrote:

Mr. Stanley commenced taking daguerreotypes of the Indians with his apparatus. They are delighted and astonished to see their likeness produced by the direct action of the sun. They worship the sun and they considered Mr. Stanley was inspired by their divinity and he thus became in their eyes a great medicine man.

A government exploration of the Great Basin of Utah in 1859, led by Captain J. H. Simpson, brought along a photographer named C.

ALBERT BIERSTADT: Sioux Village near Fort Laramie, Nebraska. This half of a stereo card was published by the firm of Bierstadt Brothers. Though most of the photographs taken by the Lander party are lost, this is considered to be one of them. Its fuzzy, primitive quality indicates that Bierstadt wisely chose painting as his true vocation. American History Division, The New York Public Library, Astor, Lenox and Tilden Foundations

C. Mills, whose work was disappointing. Simpson mentioned that similar failures had been encountered by other expeditions. "The cause," he thought, was "chiefly in the fact that the camera is not adapted to distant scenery," producing a blurred picture. It was true that most cameras were supplied with lenses intended for taking close-up studio portraits. But there were available by that time lenses with small apertures for bringing distant scenery into focus, and many photographers used them.

Another expedition in the same area in the same year had much greater success. This was the Captain F. W. Lander party, assigned to survey a road from Salt Lake City to the East. The photographers were S. F. Frost and Albert Bierstadt. They used a stereo camera and took the first stereo views of emigrant wagon trains, Indians, and camp scenes. Bierstadt saw the stereo views as useful models for his paintings, but he and his brothers Edward and Charles marketed the pictures in card stereograph form. This was the beginning of the Bierstadt Brothers firm, which later became a major manufacturer of stereo views. Their factory in New Bedford, Massachusetts, later made stereos in the hundreds of thousands.

The coming of the Civil War in 1861 brought the early period of photographing and surveying the West to a close. During the war, a whole new generation of photographers would gain experience photographing the battlefields for Mathew Brady's collection of war views. In 1865, the nation's attention turned once more to the frontier, and these new photographers would bring their cameras west.

2
PHOTOGRAPHING
THE RAILROADS

During the Civil War, photography gained a new dimension, bringing images of the horror to the non-combatants. The photographs taken by Brady and his employees drew fascinated crowds wherever they were exhibited. "These pictures have a terrible distinctness," wrote the critic for the *New York Times*. "By the aid of the magnifying glass, the very features of the slain may be distinguished."

Not only was Brady's project the first time a war was photographed on such a large scale, but the armies themselves found that photographers could be useful. Details of terrain, bridges, and railroad lines could be recorded with accuracy for study by map-makers and strategists.

The war nullified the sectional rivalry that had stymied the transcontinental railroad project. It also showed the necessity for a railroad to unite the two coasts of the country. The frontier from the Mississippi to the Rockies lay waiting for settlers, miners, and ranchers. Populating the great land mass and extracting its riches would only be possible if an efficient means of transportation existed.

With the departure of the Southern legislators, the Federal Congress passed a bill in 1862 authorizing a northern route for the railroad. Congress offered as incentives to the companies that would build the line cash payments of $16,000 per mile of track laid, plus 12,800 acres of public land for each mile of track. For track over mountainous regions, the bonus was increased to $48,000 per mile.

Two companies were given the right to build tracks. One, the Union Pacific, would build westward from Omaha. Thomas C. Durant gained control of this line through manipulation of its stock.

JOHN CARBUTT: *Samuel Reed, superintendent of construction for the Union Pacific, surveys an unfinished section of track seeming to stretch to infinity. The picture symbolizes the vast project of building the transcontinental railroad and Americans' feeling in 1865 that the frontier offered limitless opportunities.* Library of Congress

The other line, the Central Pacific, had been organized in 1861 after an engineer named Theodore Judah showed that a practicable route could be built through the Sierra Nevada Mountains by way of the Donner Pass. He persuaded four Sacramento shopowners to invest in his plan. Later known as the "Big Four," they were Charles Crocker, Mark Hopkins, Collis Huntington, and Leland Stanford. They would become fabulously wealthy from the venture.

Publicity was one means by which the men who controlled the railroads hoped to encourage new investors and settlers to the land they received from the government. The Big Four asked a fellow Sacramento businessman, photographer Alfred A. Hart, to make a series of pictures of the construction of the railroad and scenery along the route. In return, Hart was given the opportunity to sell stereo views of his pictures.

Hart began work in 1864, but he hadn't missed much. Construction on both lines was slow to get going. An incentive came in 1864 when Congress decreed that the Central Pacific would no longer be required to stop its tracks when it finished the task of crossing the Sierras. It would be allowed to build until it met the track of the Union Pacific. As soon as it dawned on the owners that this meant the faster each line built the more money it would make, construction began in earnest. Congress had laid down the rules for the greatest race ever run—with men laying iron tracks across the continent for fabulous sums of money as the prize.

A former Union general, Jack Casement, and his brother Dan were placed in charge of the construction of the Union Pacific. The Casement brothers devised new methods of construction to do the work as efficiently as possible. They took a disorganized gang of laborers, including tough Irish immigrants, Indians, ex-slaves, former soldiers, and Mormon settlers, and made them a driving force through the West.

The Casements set as a goal one mile per day, for which the men were paid $2 a day. When the goal was reached, the Casements increased it to 1½ miles a day, and then 2 miles a day, each time increasing the pay of the workers, finally to $4 a day.

By October, 1866, the Union Pacific had reached its first objective of the 100th meridian, 247 miles west of Omaha. One of the principals in the railroad, an eccentric financier with a flair for publicity named George Francis Train, organized a gala celebration of the event. He ran a special train with "two hundred and fifty of the most distinguished citizens of America" to the 100th meridian. The excursion was recorded by a Chicago photographer, John Carbutt, and his assistant T. J. Hine.

President Johnson had refused an invitation to attend the excursion, but plenty of society figures, European nobility, and newspaper men accepted. It was indeed a royal trip. The meals included trout, quail, buffalo tongue, oysters, antelope, grouse, duck, and braised bear in port wine sauce. Two brass bands were taken along to provide entertainment, and Train had prepared other surprises.

The first night out from Omaha the excursion stopped at Columbus, Nebraska, where the passengers disembarked for a night spent in tents on the Plains. A band of Pawnee Indians hired to perform a war dance entertained the travelers before they nestled into soft mattresses and buffalo robes provided to ease the discomforts of "frontier life."

The next morning, the Pawnees thrilled the passengers with a mock raid on the train and Dr. Durant grandly stepped from his car to "pacify" them with gifts of beads and trinkets. Unbeknownst to the admiring travelers, the Indians had also demanded a hundred dollars in gold, paid in advance, to provide the entertainment.

The arrival at the 100th meridian seemed somewhat anticlimactic. As Carbutt's pictures show, it was a bleak spot with only a wooden sign erected to mark it. The Casement brothers were averse to stopping work for the entertainment of the owners of the line, and were already laying track 22 miles farther down the line. The excursion continued to the end of the tracks, where the party watched the sweating gangs of workmen for a while, and then settled down to a dinner of lamb, roasted antelope, and Chinese duck, followed by champagne and fireworks.

The following day, the train stopped back at the actual site of the 100th meridian to allow the passengers to pose for an official photograph taken by Carbutt. The last night out before returning to Omaha, Train would seemingly have run out of effects to startle the jaded passengers. But his fertile brain devised a grand finale. He had a twenty-mile stretch of prairie set on fire to regale the guests watching in safety from their camp.

If publicity was the aim of the trip, Train's idea succeeded. Carbutt

48

JOHN CARBUTT: *A group of distinguished guests at the 100th meridian party, stopping for their pictures at the precise site of the 100th meridian, 247 miles west of Omaha.* Union Pacific Railroad Photo

published a set of approximately 300 stereo views of the trip, and they were enthusiastically promoted by the railroad. After they began to circulate, a sudden upsurge in investors' money began to come in. People could see with their own eyes that they were really laying track in the wilderness. Furthermore, settlers were encouraged to believe that the Indians really were rather harmless, since they could be bought off for a few trinkets. And Durant wanted to encourage this view, since he needed settlers to buy up the land the railroads were granted by the government.

Carbutt himself returned the following year to take more photo-

ALFRED A. HART: Chinese workers for the Central Pacific. Their task here, giving some idea of the enormous amount of work that went into the making of the railroad, is to fill in the valley around the temporary trestle to the top of the tracks, using only hand carts and one-horse wagons to transport the dirt. Southern Pacific Photo

graphs of the line and the Indians who inhabited the country. After that, he settled in Chicago, where he ran a successful studio for many years and became an innovator in photographic techniques. His patented portable "dark-tent," for preparing and developing collodion plates in the wilderness, was used by many of the photographers of the West, including some of the photographers with the later geological surveys. Some historians also credit Carbutt with being the first to use a celluloid base for a dry-plate photographic emulsion—in other words, he invented the "film" most cameras of the present time use.

Meanwhile, the directors of the Central Pacific faced two problems in competing with the Union Pacific's fast-moving Casement brothers. First, was a scarcity of cheap labor to construct the line. Second, was the problem of crossing the Sierra Nevadas. Tunnels would have to be blasted through the rock, and experienced railroad men expected such a task would take years. By then, the Casement brothers would have built their track clear across the West to the other side of the mountains.

Charles Crocker, directing operations, decided that he would send work crews over the mountains by wagon and set them to work on the other side building eastward as fast as possible. Somehow the tunnels through the mountain would be built and linked up with the other track when they were finished.

As for laborers, Crocker hit upon the idea of using some of the thousands of Chinese immigrants working in California. The victims of prejudice, they were forced to take menial jobs with low pay. The railroad salaries would be enticing to them. Crocker's chief of staff, J. H. Strobridge, opposed the idea. Strobridge once declared proudly, "Men generally earn their money when they work for me," and he felt that the small-statured Chinese would not live up to the work standards of a white man.

Crocker persuaded Strobridge to give fifty Chinese a trial at $35 a month. Soon Strobridge was calling for more Chinese laborers, and still more, till finally the Central Pacific was recruiting laborers in China itself, arranging for their passage to California—to be repaid out of their wages.

Public interest in the transcontinental railroad was at a fever pitch. Hart's and Carbutt's stereo sets sold in the tens of thousands. Now that the railroad could be used for travel, the scenery along its tracks was photographed by others, including Thomas Houseworth of California and Carleton Watkins. Watkins had befriended Collis Huntington when Huntington was a tinsmith in New York State. The railroad magnate arranged for Watkins to get a free lifetime pass on the line, and threw railroad photographic assignments in Watkins's way.

The Union Pacific had its own photographers, among them Andrew J. Russell and J. B. Silvis. Russell was hired in 1868. Trained as an artist, he had been a captain in the Union Army engineer corps during the Civil War. One of his chief duties had been photographing military railroads and bridges.

Many photographers, like Russell, had received their early training as painters. The role of the painter as illustrator was being superseded by the photographer. Like a blacksmith learning to repair automobiles, painters like Carvalho and Russell took up the new medium to keep abreast of the times.

But Russell's artistic eye distinguished his photographs from Hart's and many others' of lesser talent. The striking photographs that Russell took of the scenery of the Plains have a drama and immediacy that startles the eye even today. He had an uncommon talent for combining the elements of what one modern critic called "the threefold theme of men, machine, and nature."

Working from a base in Echo City, construction headquarters for the Union Pacific, Russell photographed the last 600 miles of construction along the line from Cheyenne, Wyoming, to Promontory, Utah.

Russell loaded his equipment wagon aboard Jack Casement's work train, now lengthened to eighty cars, including a complete feed store and saddle shop, kitchens, dining cars, bunk cars, a butcher's car, and so on. The train kept its own herd of cattle traveling alongside as a source of fresh meat. There were also a thousand loaded rifles aboard to be distributed to the men in case of Indian attack.

Out in front of the train, teams of "mule-whackers" hauled wooden ties to the pre-graded roadbed and dropped them. A team of men laid them in place. Another team, riding aboard a horse-drawn flatcar loaded with rails, dropped the rails over the ties, and "head-spikers" attached the rails to the ties—ten spikes per rail, three blows of the hammer to each spike. The clang of steel against steel echoed across the Plains, farther and farther west each day. Four hundred rails to a mile, 1,800 miles to San Francisco—21 million blows of a "head-spiker's" hammer.

Charles Crocker's 15,000 cone-hatted, blue-jacketed Chinese workers were at the other end of the Plains, working just as fast. During the winter, the men worked virtually every day, despite the deep snowfall of the mountain regions. Some of the time they worked in three shifts around the clock, never stopping, for not a

53

ANDREW J. RUSSELL: Citadel Rock at Green River, Wyoming, where the Casements built a temporary town as a construction headquarters. The train on the right is on a temporary trestle which was eventually replaced by the stone bridge being built on the left. Photograph Courtesy of The Oakland Museum

day could be spared. The Central Pacific built thirty-seven miles of immense snow-sheds over the tracks to keep the snow off while the men worked. Hart followed along with them, photographing it all.

In April, 1868, the Central Pacific had succeeded in driving its rails through the Sierra Nevadas, and linked up to its track on the eastern slopes. Every mile of track now completed meant an additional $16,000 and 1,280 acres of land for the line that built it. Workers for

both lines rode a hundred miles or more ahead of the actual track, surveying and grading, seeking to establish their "right" to the territory.

The advance crews for the two lines finally met, but neither stopped. Parallel to each other, the Central Pacific road graders drove east while the Union Pacific's men went westward, sometimes sabotaging each other's efforts with a well-timed dynamite

ALFRED A. HART: Snow sheds such as those shown here in the process of construction were used to keep the pace of construction going through the winter. Each day gained or lost would mean thousands of dollars more in profits or loss to the line. Southern Pacific Photo

blast. Clearly, the race had gotten out of hand, and finally President Grant called representatives of the two lines together. They settled on a point where the tracks would meet—Promontory Point, north of the Great Salt Lake and seventy miles from the Mormon city of Salt Lake. The date was set for May 10, 1869.

A few weeks before that date, Daniel Casement entered a photographer's studio in Salt Lake City to have his picture taken. It was a turning point in the career of the photographer, Charles R. Savage.

Savage had been born in 1832 in a slum in Southampton, England. He had no formal education, but read widely. He converted to Mormonism when he was fifteen, and came to the United States to work for the Church of Latter-Day Saints in 1856.

In New York City, Savage learned photography from another Church member, T. B. H. Stenhouse, who had a studio in Brooklyn. In 1860, Savage, his wife, and two young sons crossed the Plains in an ox-drawn wagon. In Salt Lake City, he entered into partnership with Marsena Cannon, and opened his own gallery when Cannon left for southern Utah. Savage took on another partner, the artist George M. Ottinger, and the firm of Savage and Ottinger soon acquired a reputation for quality.

J. B. SILVIS: Chinese section hands working near Promontory. J. B. Silvis, about whom almost nothing is known, evidently traveled along the line in the special photographic car on the right. Denver Public Library Western Collection

Savage had met both Carleton Watkins and H. T. Anthony on a trip in 1866, and profited from the advice he got from the two more experienced photographers. Eastern photography magazines began to notice Savage's work in their columns. Yet at the time Casement walked into his gallery, Savage's work was not nationally known.

Casement's visit changed that. Casement was favorably impressed by the work he saw displayed on Savage's gallery walls, and two weeks later, Col. Silas Seymour, the consulting engineer of the Union Pacific, came to ask Savage to photograph the completion of the railroad at Promontory.

It was the chance of a lifetime for Savage. The linking of the rails was awaited eagerly across the country. There was a ready-made market among the large eastern newspapers and magazines for photographs from which to make wood cuts and lithographs. Sales to the public of stereo views of the driving of the last spike would be huge.

In view of the fact that both railroads already employed photographers who would also be at the ceremony, Seymour's request may seem a little strange. But he was probably displaying a little political sense in asking a Mormon photographer to take part as well. Brigham Young, who had contributed assistance to the building of the line, was still irritated that the main road would not pass through Salt Lake City. Furthermore, the railroad had to continue to operate through territory populated only by Indians and Mormon settlers, and some Americans of the time regarded the Mormons as being almost as threatening as the Indians.

Whatever the reasons, when May 10 dawned, three photographers were on hand to record the event. Savage had arrived in the construction camp on May 7, and was invited to lunch with the Casement brothers in their private car. The scenes in the tent city that had grown up around the camp were a source of some distaste to the devout Mormon photographer. He described the scene in his diary: "I was credibly informed that twenty-four men had been killed in the several camps in the last twenty-five days. Certainly a harder set of men have never congregated together before . . . their presence would be a scourge on any community. At Blue Run the returning demons were being piled on the cars in every state of drunkenness. Every ranch or tent has whiskey for sale. Verily, the men earn their money like horses and spend it like asses!"

Savage met with Russell and Hart in the Casements' camp the following day, presumably to discuss their roles in the upcoming celebration. On the 10th, the three of them set up their cameras on the north side of the remaining gap in the tracks. Leland Stanford, representing the Central Pacific, and Thomas Durant of the Union Pacific were each to drive a golden stake into a tie made of laurel, using silver sledge hammers. Stanford's hammer was connected by wire to a telegraph key that would record the blows for the crowds waiting back east.

A team of Union Pacific workers brought up one of the two final rails, followed by blue-jacketed Chinese laborers with the other rail for the Central Pacific. Eyewitness accounts say that someone in the crowd called to Savage as the Chinese approached with the final rail: "Now's the time, Charlie! Take a shot!" The Chinese, whose command of English was slight, heard the word "shot" and drew a different interpretation. They dropped the rail and scattered, but were eventually coaxed into returning.

After prayer and speeches, the ceremony began at last. Stanford swung his sledge and missed the spike completely. Durant followed suit, and out of politeness or similar clumsiness, also missed the spike. Drunken laughter issued from the assembled crowd of track workers. The telegraph operator was quick-witted enough to operate the key manually to signal that the railroad was "Done." Back east, it was a signal for parades to begin: the one in Chicago was eight miles long.

An eyewitness said that one of the photographers actually took a shot of the men swinging the hammers, but the glass plate was broken in the crush of the crowd. Savage and Russell, standing a few feet apart, photographed similar views of the two locomotives nearly touching, with crews astride each engine waving champagne bottles. Hart seems to have climbed on top of one of the locomotives and taken a picture from that angle. Several of his pictures of the earlier construction show he was fond of this vantage point, but how he was able to handle a bulky wet-plate camera, with its slow exposure times, from that precarious position, has never been explained.

All three photographers sent photographs of the occasion to magazines back east—*Harper's Weekly* and *Leslie's Illustrated Weekly* among them—where they were copied by engravers onto the

ALFRED A. HART: *Standing astride the engine of the rival Union Pacific Line, Hart photographed the slow approach of the Union Pacific's engine toward the meeting place.* Union Pacific Railroad Photo

wooden plates used for illustration. Some years later, one of the photographs became a standard feature in American history books. Until very recently, this picture was thought to have been the one Savage took, but when the original plates were found in a dusty archive, it turned out to be Russell's.

The fate of the three photographers at Promontory tells us much about the precarious job photographing was, and why today it is so

ANDREW J. RUSSELL: Astride the engine of the Central Pacific's Jupiter, *A. J. Russell photographed the same scene, from the westward approach. The tripod of Hart's camera, resembling a crutch, can be seen on the top of the opposite engine.* Union Pacific Railroad Photo

difficult to determine the actual photographers of many early pictures. Hart died in the same year the rails were joined, at about fifty-three years of age. No one seems to have recorded the manner of his death or even given a full account of his life. It is known that his railroad stereo views, which he had issued under his own imprint from Sacramento, were obtained by C. E. Watkins. Watkins

ANDREW J. RUSSELL: *The lines meet at last, with the superintendents of construction shaking hands in the center and the crews offering bottles of champagne to each other. Not satisfied with this view, Leland Stanford, of the Central Pacific, commissioned a painter to do the "official" portrait of the scene. It shows several notables who were not actually present, including Theodore Judah, who had done the first practical survey work but who had died several years before.* Photograph Courtesy of The Oakland Museum

published them in his own series of views of the Pacific Coast. When Watkins in turn went bankrupt, the photographs fell into the hands of Isaac W. Taber, who again issued them without credit to Hart. Hart's originals are lost today, but many of the stereo cards still are found in historical societies and antique shops.

The Union Pacific issued an album of fifty of Russell's best photographs to commemorate the completion of the railroad, but Russell himself never achieved the fame he deserved. He later ran a photographic studio in New York City and contributed illustrations to *Leslie's Illustrated Weekly.*

Russell's "friend," the self-styled Professor Stephen James Sedgwick, copied Russell's photographs onto glass slides that could be projected onto a large screen with a "Magic Lantern." Sedgwick used the slides in conjunction with a series of lectures he had prepared describing an imaginary trip on the railroad from Omaha to the Pacific. Slide-and-lecture shows such as this one were popular entertainments in the nineteenth century. Sedgwick is thought to have used other photographers' work, and may have taken a few pictures himself, but the bulk of his collection came from Russell. Russell, unfortunately, didn't share in the profits from Sedgwick's tours.

Of the three photographers at Promontory, Savage alone managed to keep control of his pictures. Resting on the fame they brought him, and the income from his series of stereo views, he continued a successful career for many years.

Others besides Sedgwick and Savage made money from the public's curiosity about the new railroad. Few ordinary citizens had the money or the leisure to take the seven-day trip to the coast, but they could make their own stereopticon journeys at a nominal cost. H. T. Anthony was one of the entrepreneurs who satisfied the demand for stereo views of the railroad. He sent T. C. Roche, a former camera operator for Brady's studio, along the entire length of the road in 1870 to record several hundred views.

In Omaha in 1869 was a young man, W. H. Jackson, who would go on to become the most famous of all the early western photographers. He too would gain early recognition from his pictures of the newly completed railroad. Growing up in New England, Jackson had taught himself to draw and paint. With these skills he found work as a retoucher of photographs in several eastern studios. The wanderlust that never left him brought Jackson west in 1866. He worked as an ox-team driver, or "bullwhacker," and took on the job of driving a herd of wild mustangs to the railhead. He recorded these early western experiences in drawings but, sadly, not in photographs.

With the help of their father, Jackson and his two younger brothers bought a photographic studio in Omaha in 1867. The firm of Jackson Brothers did the standard work any town studio did at the time, taking portraits and scenes of local interest. Such work was less than satisfying to Jackson, who recalled, "I was eager to be on the road again and with my camera make a record of what was happening."

At first he satisfied his impulses by taking travelers out to the end of the track to be photographed. He also outfitted a one-horse traveling darkroom for photographing Indians and scenery around Omaha. With the completion of the railroad, Jackson decided to photograph as much of the line as he could. He left his brothers in charge of the studio while he and another Omaha photographer, Arundel C. Hull, set out along the railroad.

Jackson devised for the trip a portable darkroom that consisted of a wooden box 30" × 15" × 15" fitted with pans and trays and made so that a canopy could be attached to it for darkroom work. He and Hull had two cameras: a medium-sized (for the time) 8" × 10" plate camera and a stereo view model.

Jackson and Hull had no commission from anyone; they had to earn their living as they traveled. Their first stop was in Cheyenne, then a two-year-old town that had sprung up around one of the construction headquarters for the railroad. Jackson described its early days: "Men poured into this new railroad center . . . and immediately there was a mixed population of saloon keepers, gamblers, and their riff-raff followers, together with a host of migratory merchants, restaurant keepers, hotel men, barbers, smiths, clerks, and other working folk."

The two young photographers knew which "merchant" would be doing the biggest business, and they spent an afternoon plying the local madam with bottles of wine until she agreed to commission them to photograph her establishment and employees. Hull, the promoter of the pair, soon drummed up more business, and they had six days of steady work. The profits enabled them to buy a tent for camping along the trail. They also captured a major commission: a railroad porter ordered a thousand prints of the beautiful terrain around Weber and Echo Canyons. The porter later sold them to passengers aboard his trains.

Farther west, the pickings were slimmer, and Hull and Jackson scraped up what work they could by photographing engineers, conductors, and laborers along the line.

At Echo Canyon, Jackson met an employee of Russell's who showed him the prints Russell had made in the area. Jackson knew Russell by reputation, and met him a month later. His photographs of the canyons are frank imitations of the more experienced photographer's work.

In Salt Lake City, the pair of photographers nearly ran out of money. A few days earlier they had to borrow money from a baggage master to pay the collect freight charges on some chemicals that they badly needed. Fortunately, they were able to earn money by aggressively seeking small business that firms like Savage's disdained. Jackson's diary records: "Sent Hull up to the bridge builder's camp, and I took the ones for about town . . . at the close of the day found we had something more than thirty dollars." Jackson visited Savage's gallery, meeting Savage himself, and was annoyed at the "pretty stiff price" Savage charged for cardboard Jackson needed to mount his prints.

Jackson was careful about his money, taking the "three-dollar opposition line" instead of the more comfortable Wells Fargo stagecoach, which cost $5. But occasionally Jackson notes small extravagances: "Spent a dollar buying apricots at twenty-five cents a dozen—a great treat." And: "Sunk three dollars on a commonplace play."

Hull and Jackson's trip took them three months, covering the area between Omaha and Salt Lake City. Sales of the stereos made the summer a profitable one financially for Jackson. More importantly for his career, he met Dr. Ferdinand V. Hayden along the way. Hayden was impressed by Jackson's photographs, and the following year, he would invite Jackson along on the survey of the West that Hayden was heading.

Completion of the first transcontinental railroad was by no means the end of railroad-building in the West. Other ambitious men soon laid tracks for a Southern Pacific, a Northern Pacific, a Great Northern, and other railroads spanning the West at different latitudes. Several lines ran north and south, tying the major cities of Salt Lake City, Denver, and others, with the main east-west routes. Photographers were used by all the lines for publicity pictures, and stereo views of the new lines sold to Easterners who never seemed to tire of pictures of the frontier.

The Kansas Pacific, or as it was first called, the Union Pacific, Eastern Division, ran across Kansas on a line that would eventually run from Kansas City to Denver. A British doctor, William Bell, became a photographer along the Kansas Pacific almost as an afterthought. In 1867, he came to America to see the West and saw his chance by enlisting to travel with General William Palmer's surveying party that would map the route of the Kansas Pacific. Unfortunately, Palmer's party already had a doctor. Bell asked, almost in desperation, what skills the party *did* need. He was told it lacked a photographer, and in two weeks Bell learned enough photography to qualify. It was a fortunate move, for the original doctor soon left the party, and Bell served a dual role. He wrote a book describing his travels. It is illustrated with woodcuts made from his photographs, though few originals survive.

Bell was a keen and sophisticated observer, and his description of the effect the railroads had on settlement of the West is a classic. Each new town lying in the path of the railroad experienced a boom that could ironically be destructive. Bell wrote:

As the rails approach, the fun begins, and up goes the price of the [real estate] lots, higher and higher. At last [the town] becomes the terminal depot—the starting point for the western trade—where the goods are transferred to ox trains, and sent to Denver, to Santa Fe, Fort Union, and other points. The terminal depot quickly rises to the zenith of its glory. Town lots are bought up on all sides to build accommodation for traders, teamsters, camp-followers, and loafers, who seem to drop from the skies. This state of things lasts only for a time. The terminal depot must soon be moved forward, and the little colony will be left to its own resources. If the district has good advantages, it will remain; if not, it will disappear, and the town lots will fall to nothing.

Palmer's party linked up for part of the way with George A. Custer's Seventh Cavalry, which was then campaigning against Indians in Kansas. Bell encountered a U.S. Army sergeant, Frederick Wylyams, who was a graduate of Eton and of good English family. A "fatal alliance" in London had disgraced him, and he had run off to America. He and Bell became friends, and Bell taught Wylyams enough photography so that he could serve as Bell's assistant.

But in June, 1867, Wylyams and his troop encountered a force of Cheyennes who murdered and scalped the sergeant and several of his men. Bell wrote of his fellow Englishman: "The day on which he was killed he had promised to help me in printing off some copies of the photographs which I had taken on the way, so I had to print off my negatives alone, and to take a stereograph of him, poor fellow, as he lay: a copy of which I sent to Washington that the authorities should see how their soldiers were treated on the Plains."

Another photographer along the Kansas Pacific was Alexander Gardner, a Scotsman who had come to this country and worked as head of Mathew Brady's Washington gallery. Gardner made his first trip to America in 1849, when he and his brother-in-law established a community in Iowa called Clydesdale. The community was set up along ideal lines patterned on the teachings of Robert Owen, a British reformer and socialist. Gardner returned to Britain and brought back with him more Scottish workingmen to settle in Clydesdale.

In 1856, Gardner accompanied his wife, mother, brother James, and two young children to North America, with the intention of settling in Clydesdale for good. But on their arrival in America, they learned that an epidemic was sweeping the Iowa community. Gardner could not risk taking his family there. Instead, they went to New York City, where Gardner obtained employment in Mathew Brady's daguerreotype gallery. Gardner soon rose to a position of trust and authority. He was responsible for the gallery's many technical innovations, and when Brady opened a new gallery in the nation's capital, he put Gardner in charge.

All went well until the Civil War, when Brady decided to collect his record of the war in photographs. Brady now worked almost full-time in Washington, and he and Gardner began to have serious

ALEXANDER GARDNER: *The U.S. Express Overland Stage and Mail pre-pares to leave for Denver from the Hays City Post Office, 1867. The Kansas Pacific line didn't reach Denver until 1870, and the stage route filled in the gap. While it was the railhead, Hays was an important town, but after the*

line was completed it declined like so many other towns along the way. An armed guard of black soldiers was assigned to protect this particular shipment from possible attack. Kansas State Historical Society, Topeka

differences. One of these centered around the proper credit for photographs. Like most galleries of the time, Brady's identified a photograph with the name of the studio, not the name of the actual photographer. Gardner and apparently several others wanted credit for their work, and when Brady refused it Gardner set up his own studio. Several Brady employees, notably the brilliant Timothy H. O'Sullivan, joined Gardner. Later, Gardner became an official photographer for the Army of the Potomac.

At the war's end, the Iowa community had relocated to McGregor, Iowa, and was again thriving. Gardner's adopted daughter lived there, and he had sent some of his family there during the war. Gardner himself had found time to make several visits to the area, and may have taken some pictures then.

In 1867, Gardner became disenchanted with Washington gallery work and went west with a wagon equipped for taking wet-plate pictures. He made an extensive series of stereo views along the line of the Kansas Pacific, including a spur that went from Lawrence to Leavenworth.

Many of the photographs Gardner took in 1867 are important in tracing the development of early Kansas towns. The early cattle towns of Ellsworth and Hays were photographed by Gardner soon after they sprang up at the railhead. His photographs of forts and Indians in the area are also prized historical records.

Oddly, for sheer drama, his pictures along the Kansas Pacific— numbering about 150 stereo views—are not nearly as effective as his striking views of the battlefields of the war. Part of the drab quality of his Kansas pictures is no doubt due to the fact that Kansas, as a natural setting, does not compare with the beautiful scenery that Russell photographed along the Union Pacific or that Hart viewed in the Sierras.

Gardner seems to have been overwhelmed by the vast spaces of the prairie. He noted on his stereo cards the distance to the far background. Many times, he appears to have backed up as far as he could and recorded a town or fort that appears as a stark line of buildings rising slightly above the prairie. Stereo views, however, are always at a disadvantage when viewed "flat," without the assistance of a stereoscope. In three dimensions, some of Gardner's views show that he aimed for a deep perspective to highlight the grandeur of distant vistas.

Later, Gardner went back to Washington and set up a rogue's gallery of criminal photographs for the Metropolitan Police Department. It was one of the first examples of photography used for this purpose. Gardner's real estate investments brought him a comfortable old age before his death in 1882.

Probably the limit in elegant accommodations for a railroad photographer was reached by Frank J. Haynes, well known for his photographs of Yellowstone National Park. In 1876, Haynes was a young Minnesota-based photographer working in the area served by the then-building Northern Pacific Railroad. Haynes took some photographs of Northern Pacific trains and stations that impressed a superintendent of the line. The superintendent assigned Haynes to take pictures along the existing line in return for $2 a day plus materials and free transportation.

Haynes's work was so satisfactory that in 1880 or 1881 he was appointed the official photographer for the line, which reached from Minneapolis-St. Paul across North Dakota, Montana, Idaho, and Washington to the Pacific. Haynes proposed that the railroad equip and lease him a Pullman studio car to hold his laboratory and equipment. The railroad agreed, and the "Haynes Palace Car" came into being. It was a rolling darkroom, studio, business office, and apartment, equipped with a kitchen and cook. The cook, according to one account spiced with photographic terms, was "an expert operator who can pose an antelope steak on a dry-plate in the highest style of the art."

A journalist, after a visit to the Palace Studio Car, called it "glittering. . . . No gilt-encircled, gold-emblazoned circus car can compare with this paragon of brilliant beauty." Haynes estimated that the car cost $13,000, a small fortune at the time. In it, he traveled wherever the line ran, taking photographs of the railroad as well as settlements, military posts, miners, and Indians along the route.

The money for Haynes's car was well spent, for Haynes's photographs were useful in publicizing the line among tourists, investors, and potential settlers. The railroad published a series of brochures, some of them a hundred pages long, illustrated with Haynes photographs and titled *Wonderland*.

Haynes did accompany what was probably the most disastrous trip in the history of the building of the railroads. It was intended to be a triumphal tour, in 1883, celebrating the laying of the last tie in

FRANK J. HAYNES: Henry J. Villard, the hatless man on the side of the locomotive, proudly begins the triumphal tour of the completed Northern Pacific railroad that was to end in financial disaster for him and the line. The Haynes Foundation

the Northern Pacific that would unite Minnesota with Puget Sound in Washington. Henry Villard, the latest in a series of presidents of the Northern Pacific, had finally succeeded in driving the line through to the coast, eleven years after it had reached Fargo. To celebrate the achievement, he ran a special train with more than 350 guests, including former President Grant; General Phil Sheridan, Commander-in-Chief of the Army; Carl Schurz, former Secretary of the Interior; and William M. Evarts, former Secretary of State. Germany and Britain had sent official representatives. Most im-

72

portantly, aboard the train were scores of wealthy men who held stock in the railroad.

The windows of the cars on the train were washed frequently throughout the trip, to allow the guests to see the scenery. Unfortunately, what they saw seemed to them to be a bleak, unpromising wilderness, quite unlike the "wonderland" scenery that Haynes's eye had caught with his camera. As the special train progressed from St. Paul to Bismarck, Glendive, Miles City, Billings, and points west, the stockholders became uneasy. "My God," one of them is

Routes Westward: The Oregon Trail and the early transcontinental railroads.

quoted as saying, "this is a damned desert!" The Indians that Villard had arranged to meet the train, unlike the Indians of the 100th meridian excursion, appeared fierce and, to quote another passenger, "one howling, yelling, leaping mass of painted and feathered savages." As the train made its frequent stops at towns along the line to acknowledge the cheers of the western frontier citizens, some of the stockholders began to slip off to the nearest telegraph office, sending a message back to the East: "Sell Northern Pacific stock." By the time the train finished its triumphal tour Northern Pacific stock had plummeted on Wall Street, and a hostile group of investors took control of the line and excluded Villard, almost at the moment when he was officiating at the "last spike" ceremonies. It took Villard years to recoup the money, and his railroad, lost by that fatal trip.

The building of the railroads that spanned the West was the greatest engineering feat of the nineteenth century. Completion of the line meant the destruction of the way of life of the Indian inhabitants of the country. But the railroad brought a population of farmers and ranchers that filled up the area between the Mississippi and the Pacific. Americans felt a tremendous pride in their achievement, augmented by the fact that they could see the lines progress and see the frontier being tamed. Photographers promoted and glorified the work, making as they did so a permanent record that later generations can look back on and ponder.

3
PHOTOGRAPHING
THE GREAT SURVEYS

In the period from 1867 to 1878, four major scientific expeditions explored and mapped large areas of the West. As the country's energies turned from war to the building of the transcontinental railroad, there was a need to fill in the gaps in the maps of the West and establish the location of mineral wealth to encourage investment and settlement in the frontier areas. The scientific expeditions that accomplished these tasks are known as the Four Great Surveys. When their work was done, the West would have ceased to be a mystery.

The leaders of the four surveys were extraordinary men. Each had qualities of the adventurer and the scientist. Each used the power of publicity to wring the necessary funds for their costly expeditions from a skeptical Congress. Each brought along photographers whose pictures of the surveys' work would fan public enthusiasm and reveal the West as it actually was.

The work of the survey photographers is particularly valuable to us today. Because their photographs were made for scientific purposes, virtually all of them are identified with full details of place and date. They show us a major part of the West when it was pristine and unspoiled. Some of the scenery they photographed was later marred by mining operations and settlements. Whole canyons have since been flooded by the backwaters of modern dams. The survey photographers show us the West as it was in the 1870s.

1

Early in the year 1867, three of the survey leaders-to-be—Clarence King, Ferdinand Hayden, and John W. Powell—were in Washington, D.C., seeking funds for their proposed expeditions. Of the three, Clarence King had the most survey experience. After graduation from Yale four years earlier, King and his friend James Terry Gardner had joined the California Geological Survey, headed by Josiah Whitney. For nearly four years, King participated in the Whitney survey, learning the practical work of scientific exploration.

He also saw the value of photography to a survey, when Carleton E. Watkins joined the group in 1866 for a trip with King and Gardner to explore the Yosemite area. *The Yosemite Book,* as the report of that part of the survey is known, contained fifty of Watkins's photographs. A special edition was distributed to influential politicians, and it is likely that Watkins's dramatic photographs made more of an impression on them than the technical language of the report.

In 1866, while King and Gardner were on a high Sierra peak, looking out over hundreds of miles of unexplored terrain to the east, King made a decision. He would attempt to organize a survey grander than any yet accomplished. It would explore the 40th parallel from the Plains to the Pacific.

By the following spring, King had rallied the support of influential members of the scientific community for his proposal. Even so, King's well-wishers doubted he could muster the political skills necessary to wring money from Congress. King's idea for a major survey of the western Plains was far from unique, and leadership of such a survey would be a political plum.

But King prevailed, and came away from Washington with the title Geologist in Charge of the U.S. Geological Exploration of the 40th Parallel. He immediately proved himself a keen judge of talent by appointing to his expedition some of the best young scientists in the country—men who went on to distinguished careers in many fields. One of the men he selected was Timothy H. O'Sullivan, as the expedition's photographer.

O'Sullivan was then about twenty-five years old. His parents had emigrated to the U.S. from Ireland in 1842, the year of his birth. Timothy's boyhood was spent on Staten Island, not yet part of the city of New York just across the bay. But at an early age, O'Sullivan found work in Manhattan as an apprentice in the famous and elegant photograph studio of Mathew Brady.

O'Sullivan was still in Brady's employ when the Civil War broke out and Brady began collecting his views of the battlefields and men of the war. O'Sullivan proved himself a master photographer in this effort. He was not to get full credit for his work, however, until he broke with Brady and went to work for Alexander Gardner's new studio. The value of O'Sullivan's work to both Brady and Gardner can be seen from Gardner's book, *A Photographic Sketchbook of the Civil War.* It contained a hundred photographs by Gardner and his co-workers. Forty-two were credited to O'Sullivan.

O'Sullivan's experience well qualified him for the post of expedition photographer. He had been under fire several times in the war. His camera was destroyed by a shell at Bull Run. He was a man used to photographing under hardships.

In early May, 1867, the members of the expedition set sail from New York for Panama, where they crossed the Isthmus by train and sailed up the Pacific Coast to San Francisco. They collected supplies for the expedition in Sacramento, their jumping-off place.

For his work on the King survey, O'Sullivan selected a Civil War army ambulance as his traveling darkroom. In addition, he was assigned a mule and experienced "packer" to take him and his equipment where no wagon could go. On O'Sullivan's side trips, this mule carried as much as 200 pounds of photographic chemicals, plates, and equipment. When he was away from his ambulance darkroom, O'Sullivan used the portable darkroom invented by John Carbutt, which was a large canopied box on a tripod. The photographer could insert his head and arms within the box to prepare and develop the collodion plates.

On July 3, O'Sullivan, King, and some others set out from Sacramento for the base camp at Glendale, Nevada. Along the way, they stopped at Virginia City, where the rich Comstock Mine was producing silver in fabulous amounts. O'Sullivan was probably aware of the startling photographs made at Mammoth Cave in Kentucky the year before by Charles Waldack of Cincinnati. Waldack burned magnesium powder in front of large reflectors to make the first photographs of the interior of a cave.

Now O'Sullivan seized the opportunity to take his equipment into the Comstock mine and photograph the miners at work. This seems to have been a spur-of-the-moment decision, and a dangerous one

81

at that. Burning magnesium could have ignited mine dust or a pocket of gas and killed both photographer and miners. Nevertheless, O'Sullivan's luck held, and he emerged with the first photographs of an underground mine. King used the photographs in his report to emphasize the possibility of other mineral deposits awaiting exploitation.

O'Sullivan and King reached the base camp on the 15th of July. Two days later came an escort of twenty mounted troopers of the Eighth Cavalry that the army assigned to protect the King expedition.

King divided his group into smaller parties for preliminary studies. On one of these O'Sullivan and two companions took a small sailboat, the *Nettie,* down the Truckee River to explore its outlet, Pyramid Lake. The boat proved unstable in the rough rapids and sharp underwater rocks of the Truckee. At one point, the *Nettie* lay jammed between two rocks in mid-rapids. The oars were swept away, and the boat, with most of O'Sullivan's precious equipment, was in danger of being dashed to pieces by logs rushing down the turbulent stream.

O'Sullivan, described as "a swimmer of no ordinary power," stripped and jumped into the water. Battered by the rushing stream and the rocks, he made it to shore a few hundred yards downstream. Running back up the bank he called for the others to throw him a rope.

They did so, and in the confusion, they used O'Sullivan's wallet as a weight for the end of the rope. The wallet was heavy because it contained $300 in $20 gold pieces, most of O'Sullivan's pay. He was only able to watch horrified as the wallet came loose and sank in the

TIMOTHY H. O'SULLIVAN: Deep within the Comstock Mine, a worker chips away at the rock. Though O'Sullivan's magnesium flare lighted the scene well enough for a picture (as indicated by the glare at the upper right edge and reflected light from the rocks at bottom), the miner's only light usually came from the candle propped against the tool at the bottom. National Archives

TIMOTHY H. O'SULLIVAN: The eerie black deposits of tufa that give Pyramid Lake its name. Coming upon the deserted scene exhausted and nearly drowned, O'Sullivan set up his camera and made one of the brilliant, other-worldly photographs that are so typical of his unique photographic eye. National Archives

stream. "That was rough," recalled O'Sullivan, "for I never found that 'dust' again, though I prospected a long time, barefooted, for it."

The boat and its passengers and equipment were saved through O'Sullivan's quick action. The next morning, the explorers proceeded more cautiously down river, controlling the boat with ropes from the shore. Soon they came to Pyramid Lake.

Pyramid Lake had an other-worldly aura that the travelers found

eerie. It is actually the remnant of a much larger lake that existed in prehistoric times, and receives its name from two large deposits of tufa (spongy volcanic rock) that rise above the surface of the lake water like pyramids. The larger pyramid juts 500 feet above the water and to O'Sullivan it looked like a "vegetable growth of vast size."

The explorers landed the boat on the larger pyramid and clambered up its sides. O'Sullivan set up his camera and took a photograph of his two companions. Suddenly some earlier inhabitants of the rock made their prior claim known. Hissing and rattling from every crevice marked the indignation of a great number of disturbed rattlesnakes. The human invaders beat a hasty retreat, with no injuries except to dignity.

When O'Sullivan and the others regrouped at King's base camp, they found illness and other trouble had struck. "Mountain ail" (which was their name for the little-understood malarial fever) had infected a number of the party. The mounted troopers had begun to slip off as deserters. Those who remained questioned the judgment of King and the other civilian "Easterners."

Nevertheless King pushed the band onward, to the area known as the Humboldt Sink. A "sink" is a low-lying area slow to absorb the water that drains there and collects in large, stagnant pools. In the Humboldt Sink, the great pools were breeding grounds for millions of mosquitoes. Clouds of them were so thick that they snuffed out candles at night. The travelers were unaware that it was in fact the mosquitoes that carried the "mountain ail," but they were all too conscious of the bites of the ever-present voracious insects.

There were other agonies. In the open country of the sink the heat became intense. The party suffered from a lack of fresh water, and the men were afraid to drink the sulphurous, evil-smelling water that lay all around them. Going overland to escape the deadly sink was dangerous, for the terrain was composed of hills of odd, rectangular rocks, like piles of giant matchsticks. Even the sure-footed mules suffered falls, and the party struggled to escape the area.

O'Sullivan, recounting all these difficulties, retained his photographer's enthusiasm for the subject. He remarked, "It was a pretty location to work in, and *viewing* there was as pleasant work as could be desired."

King had to move north to a mining town, where the local jail was converted into an infirmary for those of the expedition laid low by malaria. At one time, out of fifty men all but three were ill.

King rallied his sick and rebellious force, and pressed farther on into the mountains. They passed through pine forests, more of the deadly "sinks," and across treacherous mountain passes. In the mountains, O'Sullivan recalled, "the party endured indescribable hardships." The summer sun made the snow drifts—in places thirty to forty feet deep—too soft for travel. The expedition could only move the heavily laden mules at night when the temperature fell rapidly and a crust of ice formed on top of the snow.

Even then, they had to move at a snail's pace to avoid thin spots in the ice, advancing on one occasion less than two and a half miles in thirteen hours. Mules suddenly fell through the ice, disappearing from sight, and frantic efforts were made to pull them out before they suffocated.

O'Sullivan's photographic eye was always open, and he was able to make a series of beautiful pictures of isolated mountain lakes formed by melting snow even during the terrifying passage through the mountains.

Finally, King moved his men back to Virginia City. The winter of 1867–68 was spent there and in Carson City, thirteen miles away. Though the field work of the first year was over, the survey's work went on year round. In the winter, specimens were assembled and classified and field notes had to be transformed into maps and reports.

O'Sullivan's winter too was a busy one, for he had to make prints of his negatives, marking each one for later use in the reports. The work of printing a photograph was arduous. The photographic paper of the time was coated with silver nitrate and egg albumen (giving the positive image the name "albumen print"). It required long, intense exposures of light to make a print on albumen paper. The negative glass plate and a blank piece of sensitized paper were placed together in a frame and exposed to the sun. The photographer had to keep watch on the paper to check the degree of development. An image would appear in about a half hour, and the paper was then removed and placed in a series of chemical baths to "fix" the image, tone it, and wash away the chemicals. Making a single print took about one hour. When one considers that in a later year of the surveys O'Sullivan was charged with making 2,500 prints and that he had no darkroom helpers, some idea of the work involved becomes clear.

King took a portfolio of O'Sullivan's 18" × 24" prints of the first year's trip and went east. He showed them to Congressmen and scientists, persuading them to finance and support the next year's survey work.

King's mission was successful, and in the spring of 1868 the survey party set out again, as it would each year through 1872. O'Sullivan photographed with King through 1869. A. J. Russell and Carleton Watkins were two of the photographers who contributed their efforts to King's survey in later years.

One of the remarkable aspects of O'Sullivan's western photographs is that though they were taken for scientific purposes, they are among the most artistically pleasing photographs ever taken of the West. O'Sullivan was a master of the technical aspects of photography, but so were many others. It was his uncanny ability to find the right place to *view* a scene, to frame it on the plate, to find just that angle and light that would create a *mood*, that makes him an artist as well as a picture-taker.

The mood in O'Sullivan's photographs is very often one of mystery and awe at the massive quality of the scenery. Even in the photographs that include human figures, the people are almost always overwhelmed, nearly swallowed up in the hard, stark features of the terrain.

One of O'Sullivan's most famous photographs was taken on the second year of the King expedition. O'Sullivan, apparently alone, left the main party, which was working its way toward the Great Salt Lake, where it would spend its second winter.

O'Sullivan took the army ambulance and four mules and struck out for the south, where great mounds of sand created by desert whirlwinds offered the opportunity for some fine pictures. O'Sullivan's account says he was "tired of *too* much high rocky," but it may have been that after a winter with the other members of the survey, he was tired of them as well.

Another member of the party offered a description of the photographer in a letter: "One would think he had slept with Grant and Meade and was the direct confidant of Stanton." The writer no doubt referred to O'Sullivan's habit of recounting his experiences in the Civil War. His braggadocio may have amused the others, but in fact O'Sullivan *was* on the scene recording Grant and his staff deliberating plans of attack. He had seen the battles and listened to the generals, while most of the other young men of King's survey had avoided the war altogether. Most of them were well educated at the best universities of the United States and Europe and O'Sullivan had no formal education to speak of.

So when he struck out on his own for a time, it may have been with a sense of relief, though there was danger in traveling without an escort through territory inhabited by Indians of uncertain temper and white men who eked out a lonely existence through any means that offered.

O'Sullivan's great picture of the sand dunes near Carson Sink has a terrifying sense of loneliness that is heightened by the ambulance and mules, black against the brilliantly white dunes, standing as if abandoned by a stranger. A set of footprints leads from the black ambulance toward the camera's point of view. The man who looked through the viewing screen and opened the shutter showed us more than mules and sand; he told us something about his own soul.

2

If O'Sullivan represented the classic loner, William Henry Jackson had another kind of temperament—outgoing, restless, and impulsive. As we have seen, Jackson's season of photographing along the frontier brought him into contact with Ferdinand V. Hayden. Hayden was a doctor of medicine who served as a Union surgeon in the war, but his real loves were paleontology and geology.

In 1867, when Nebraska became a state, Congress appropriated $5,000 for a geological survey of the newest member of the Union. Political friends helped Hayden obtain the post of geologist in charge of the survey. Hayden's skills in science and public relations would eventually expand the survey far beyond the boundaries of Nebraska in an eleven-year project that covered the West from the Dakotas to Montana and south into New Mexico, costing $690,000.

The first three years of the Hayden survey were relatively modest, but when Hayden came west in July, 1870, for the fourth year, he stopped in the Jackson Brothers studio in Omaha. The visit would have far-reaching implications for the Hayden survey and for Jackson's career.

Jackson already had more than enough work in the studio, for his brothers had left to take up farming. Even though Hayden's fourth-year budget was $25,000, he offered Jackson nothing but expenses "and," Jackson remembered the canny doctor saying, "the satisfaction I think you would find in contributing your art to science." Jackson's wife came into the office at that moment, and on being told of the offer, just laughed—"and I knew," wrote Jackson, "that everything, so far as she was concerned, was arranged." If he misinterpreted his wife's laughter, she never corrected him, and she ran the studio herself that summer, making the money to support the family while Jackson set out with Hayden.

Jackson provided his own equipment for the first year's work. It included a double-lensed stereo camera and a small-sized plate camera that made plates 6½" x 8½". Like O'Sullivan he used an army ambulance equipped with a darkroom. His working kit, containing the supplies he would need to make a picture quickly, was carried on a mule he dubbed Hypo, after the photographic stabilizing chemical.

The expedition departed from Cheyenne, Wyoming, on August 7, 1870, with twenty men, four wagons, and two army ambulances. It was to explore the territory north of the Union Pacific on the way out, with Ft. Bridger as the destination. On the return trip, the party would swing south of the railroad line.

Jackson made many side trips away from the main party, photographing both the terrain and the Indians. Much of this region was familiar to him from his trip made with Hull the year before. Only a few years earlier, he had chased wild mustangs through the same territory.

The expedition of 1870 was uneventful. It was straight scientific work—collecting fossils, mapping, noting geologic formations, and gathering mineral specimens. "But for me," Jackson wrote, "the expedition was priceless—it gave me a career." By the time the party returned to Ft. Sanders, at Laramie, Hayden had been thoroughly impressed with Jackson's skill—so much so that he offered him a permanent post as photographer to the U.S. Geological Survey (as Hayden's group was now known) at $150 a month.

The following year Jackson's camera would focus on more spectacular scenery. Hayden intended to explore the still mysterious area along the Yellowstone River. In 1869 and 1870, two small parties of explorers had gone into the region and confirmed some of the strange stories that Indians and mountain men had told for years. But Hayden would bring back scientific reports of the Yellowstone region. Jackson's photographs would show once and for all just what *did* exist in the valley of the Yellowstone. Also accompanying the party was Thomas Moran, a well-known painter, whose pictures would glorify the Yellowstone Valley, and whose knowledge of composition and light would influence Jackson's photography.

At the beginning of the trip, Hayden made an unusual request of Jackson. He wanted Jackson to bring along equipment and supplies to make prints in the field of the plates from Jackson's new 8" × 10" view camera. Such a practice was almost unheard of among the expedition photographers because of the difficulty in carrying the extra supplies and because of the time print-making required. But Hayden wanted to return from the expedition with prints in hand, so he could travel immediately to Washington to present them to Congress and the public. As Jackson shrewdly commented: "Hayden knew that Congress would keep on with its annual appropriations exactly as long as the people were ready to foot the bill, and he was determined to make them keep on wanting to."

The Yellowstone region proved to be everything Hayden had hoped for. Wonder after wonder unfolded to the scientists— surrounded by spectacular mountain peaks, the Yellowstone held spectacular geysers shooting boiling water hundreds of feet into the air, bubbling hot springs of sulfurous water, multicolored rock formations, and miles of spectacular scenery.

Jackson wrote of the excitement he and the other members of the party felt: "[Yellowstone] was regarded as a wonderland, of which a small portion only had been explored . . . everyone was sure that still more marvelous things were yet to be found. It was this expectation that gave the keenest zest to each day's journey. . . . Here was the first really important work for both scientist and picture men . . . a subject never before described or photographed."

Jackson discovered one great advantage of the region for a photographer: the water in the bubbling pools ranged from 120°F. to boiling point. Jackson found the hot water very useful for washing his plates and for quick drying of the negatives.

In some places, the water was not so accessible. Seeking a vantage point from which to photograph the falls of the Yellowstone, Jackson hauled his equipment to the top of a rocky hill. The nearest water was 200 feet below. Jackson had to make his picture and

WILLIAM H. JACKSON: The Hayden expedition on its way to the valley of the Yellowstone in 1871. The horse-drawn "cart" in the middle is actually an odometer, used to measure the trails and distances the party traveled. National Archives

immediately wrap the moist plate in wet blotting paper and towels, protecting the image with a dark cloth, to keep the plate from drying. He then slid down the hill to the stream to develop and wash the plate. Then he had to climb to the top again to begin preparations for the next shot. It took Jackson half a day's work to make four pictures.

Jackson drove himself tirelessly. "There was such an infinite variety of detail," he wrote, "that one exposure after another could be made with but little variation in the view." Jackson profited from Moran's frequent help and advice as to the best vantage point for taking a picture. Somehow, he even found time to make the prints for Hayden.

Hayden was the right man to publicize such an amazing discovery. Triumphantly, he presented the members of Congress with an album filled with Jackson's pictures, titled *Yellowstone's Scenic Wonders*. Wherever Hayden displayed the prints for the public, immediate acclaim and amazement followed. The public's enthusiasm led Congress to pass a bill setting aside the Yellowstone area for preservation as the first national park.

Jackson issued a set of stereo views from the trip, and these added to his growing fame. Yet the character of Jackson was such that he never rested on his laurels. He always was an experimenter, looking for a new challenge. He returned to Yellowstone twice more as a member of Hayden's survey, in 1872 and 1875, each time trying for better effects. He brought bigger and bigger cameras each time, as if the sheer grandeur of the scenery could only be captured by a mammoth, almost life-sized picture. In 1872, he brought an 11" × 14" camera, and in 1875 he and the mules somehow carried through the wilderness a camera fitted with 20". × 24" glass plates.

Photographing Yellowstone would have been a career for a lesser photographer. And, indeed, Jackson at times wanted to reopen his gallery and promote his stereo card business full-time. But Hayden cajoled him into the field year after year, and the list of photographs Jackson made—many times of scenery never before photographed—reads like a catalog of the wonders of the West.

After revisiting Yellowstone the following year, Jackson trained his mammoth camera on the spectacular Grand Teton Mountains, trekking through treacherous snow-covered passes to make his

Yellowstone R.

▽ Yellowstone Valley

▽ Grand Teton Mts.

▽ Fremont Peak

Pyramid Lake

▽ Humboldt Sink

kee R.

● **Virginia City**

Salt Lake City ●

■ **Ft. Bridger**   **Cheyenne**
●

Green R.

Colorado R.   **Denver**
●
▽ Mt. of the
Holy Cross
▽
▽ Pike's Peak

Virgin R. ● **Kanab**

▽ Mesa Verde

Marble Canyon

Grand
Canyon

▽
Canyon de Chelly

Little
Colorado R.

Colorado R.

M.   500

├──────────────────────────────────┤

Km.   500

The Great Surveys: Survey sites visited by photographers.

plates, the first ever taken of the range. The Grand Tetons too would become a national park in the twentieth century.

In 1873, another triumph awaited Jackson. He spent the early part of the season making photographs of the high mountains of Colorado, including a panoramic view showing the range from Long's Peak to Pike's Peak, a distance of over a hundred miles. Later, he joined the main Hayden party, which was seeking another legendary spot—the Mountain of the Holy Cross.

Explorers told of the mountain peak in Colorado that had a gigantic cross of snow on its side. The tale captured public imagination, but no one had proved that such a mountain existed. Hayden, with his keen sense of publicity, wanted to find it. Jackson, traveling overland with two others, was the first member of the party to sight the mountain. Clouds descended over the peak before he could take a picture, and he and his assistants huddled all night on the spot,

sleeping on the stony ground. In the morning, Jackson took eight pictures, washing the plates with melted snow.

Jackson took many pictures of the Indian tribes in the area explored by the Hayden survey. In 1874, he photographed a band of Uncompahgre Utes at the Los Pinos Indian Agency. When Jackson first made an attempt to photograph them, their medicine men were insistent: "No bueno," they said. "Make squaw die, papoose die, pony die, all die." Even when Jackson tried to take a distant photograph of the village, several Indians came to stand, backs to the camera, to block the view. They kicked out the legs from Jackson's tripod, tossed a blanket over the camera, and otherwise impeded him. Jackson was persistent, and made a few pictures on the sly, refusing to surrender the plates when the Indians saw what he had done.

Finally a chief called Billy informed the photographer that he was

WILLIAM H. JACKSON: At the summit of Berthoud Pass, looking north toward Middle Park in Colorado, Jackson made one of his best photographs, capturing the spirit of the lone explorer surveying the wilderness. The man with the gun is Harry Yount, game hunter for the Hayden survey and the first ranger of Yellowstone National Park. National Archives

not to continue his journey. "It would be dangerous for us to proceed farther with my strange box of bad medicine," Jackson recalled the chief telling him.

Deciding to make an impression so that there would be no further trouble, Jackson motioned to his two assistants. They were crack shots, and "I got them to put on a little exhibition of target shooting, in which I also joined." The Indians observed the demonstrations, and left Jackson alone after that.

Journeying south, Jackson reached the head of the Rio Grande River, where he met three prospectors, who told him of Indian cliff ruins that were reported to exist down by the La Plata River.

The description the miners gave, and the name of the place—*Mesa Verde*, Spanish for "green tableland"—attracted Jackson, and he persuaded one of the miners to guide the party to the spot. On September 9, 1874, the group was riding through the deepest part of Mancos Canyon. The prospector pointed to the ruins on the side of a cliff 800 feet above. Jackson and his group, which included a journalist, Ernest Ingersoll, immediately began to attempt to climb to the top of the cliff.

After 600 feet, all the others had turned back, but Jackson and Ingersoll continued climbing as the sun fell and the light waned. They used a dead tree to push each other to handholds in the rock. Finally they stood in the deserted pueblo, feeling the sensation of being the first white men ever to look down into the canyon from the ancient dwelling.

Timothy O'Sullivan had photographed similar ruins in the Canyon de Chelly, farther to the west, the preceding year. But Jackson's pictures, along with Ingersoll's dispatches to the New York *Tribune*, captured public attention as O'Sullivan's views had not. Ingersoll's description of "hieroglyphics" on the walls (photographed by Jackson) and speculations on the use of one large building as a temple encouraged public opinion that the Lost Cities of Cibola had at last been found. "The most outstanding feature for the world was that these cities had died," Jackson wrote.

In 1875, Jackson returned to Mesa Verde with his 20" × 24" camera to record additional views. He also made many pictures of the Navajo Indians, who were still living in some of the pueblos in the Moquis country.

The Centennial of the United States was the following year, and the great Exposition in Philadelphia that marked the anniversary was a triumphal tour for Jackson. Hayden appointed him to be one of the official representatives of the survey, and Jackson spent the winter making a huge model of the Mesa Verde ruins. Its popularity as an exhibit at the fair was only exceeded by the remarkable invention of Dr. Alexander Bell—the telephone. Jackson also won seven medals for the photographs he displayed.

At the Exposition, Jackson became fascinated by the new photographic materials on display. Using one idea, he constructed a camera that could take a 360-degree panoramic picture. To provide a flexible plate for taking pictures on the camera, he used rubber-coated paper as a base for the collodion emulsion.

Jackson's interest in experimentation caused a catastrophe in 1877, when he was once again in the field with Hayden. He brought with him plates on "sensitive negative tissue" using a new dry-plate process. The advantages of the new process were potentially great. Plates would no longer have to be coated and developed in the field, and the tissue negatives were far lighter than the old glass plates.

Using the new process, Jackson made over 400 pictures of the friendly Indian tribes between Santa Fe and the Moquis pueblos. When he came back to Washington to develop them, he found that every single one was blank. Jackson called it the most costly setback of his career.

Jackson was persistent. The next year, he used another kind of dry-plate emulsion when he climbed Fremont Peak to make a picture from the summit. This time he developed the pictures the following day, and found to his delight that they were acceptable.

Dry plates led eventually to the film used in modern cameras, and the invention of sensitive bromide paper made enlarged prints from small negatives possible. In the next century, for his ninetieth birthday, Jackson was given a Leica camera, weighing little more than a pound, which uses a 1" × 1½" negative from which huge enlargements can be made. Jackson weighed the camera reflectively in his hand, and commented: "This little thing makes a sport of our labors."

Rather than joining the new U.S. Geological Survey consolidated in 1879, Jackson went into business for himself with a new studio in

WILLIAM H. JACKSON: Though an assistant snapped the shutter, Jackson composed this photograph of himself with one of his mammoth cameras on Overhanging Rock, above Yosemite Valley. This was in the 1880s, after he had left the Hayden survey. Denver Public Library Western History Department

Denver. He began yet another career, which will be outlined in Chapter Five. But he would recall the survey years with affection, and write: "If any work that I have done should have value beyond my own lifetime, I believe it will be the happy labors of the decade 1869–1879."

All the survey leaders were strong-willed men, but none more so than John Wesley Powell. Born in 1834 in Mt. Morris, New York, the son of a Wesleyan preacher, Powell had little formal education. Yet he educated himself in natural history through reading and exploring neighboring states. He traveled as far west as Missouri collecting shells, minerals, and plants.

Came the Civil War, Powell enlisted in the Illinois volunteers and was commissioned a lieutenant. At the Battle of Shiloh, his right arm was blown away by a minie ball. He remained in the army till 1865, earning the rank of major, by which he was known till the end of his life.

After the war he taught at Wesleyan University in Illinois. He obtained a bequest from the state legislature to start a museum collection at the university. In the spring of 1867, he went to Washington, D.C., to seek government aid for an exploration of Colorado. As has been seen, both Hayden and King, more skilled at obtaining government grants, were there at the same time. Powell was only able to get promises of wagons, livestock, camp equipment, and surveying tools from the War Department and the Smithsonian Institution. Aided by monetary grants from Illinois colleges, Powell embarked on his exploration.

The first year's work convinced Powell that he could take an exploring party down the rugged Colorado River, which had never been explored along its full length. He raised sufficient money for a ten-month expedition, setting out in May, 1868. The river proved to be a deadly trap, and Powell and his party had to overcome the loss of a boat, treacherous rapids, and near-starvation. Three men left the party, to be killed by Indians in the wilderness. On August 29, the expedition came to a halt at a Mormon settlement near the mouth of the Virgin River.

What seemed like failure to Powell unexpectedly gained him the publicity he needed. The deaths of the three members of the expedition had been exaggerated in the newspapers to the loss of the entire party. When Powell and the others emerged safely, they were heroes. Powell spent the following year lecturing and enhancing his reputation as an intrepid explorer of the West. Congress

bestowed on him $12,000 to complete the survey of the Colorado River and its tributaries.

What became known as the Powell survey did not begin until 1871. It would cover nine years of field work, during which Powell explored most of what is today Arizona, Utah, and the western parts of Colorado and New Mexico, as well as sections of California and Wyoming.

Powell used photographers to record the work of his major

E. O. BEAMAN: The "first camp" of the Powell expedition, in the willows at Green River, Wyoming Territory. The cloth "umbrella" on a tripod to the right was set up to throw more light on the figures in shadow underneath the canopy. Even so, there was insufficient light on them to make a satisfactory picture. National Archives

surveys. He began the survey of 1871 with E. O. Beaman, an employee of the stereo card publishing firm of E. & H. T. Anthony. Powell agreed to let Anthony publish stereo views of the expedition.

On May 22, 1871, Powell's group set out from Green River in three boats, named the *Emma Dean,* the *Nellie Powell,* and the *Cañonita.* Each boat carried four men, along with supplies and the personal kit of each man. The Major, in the lead boat, rode on an armchair strapped to the top of the small cabin in the middle of the deck. He gave hand signals to the pilots of the two following boats when he sighted rapids. In quiet times, the Major read aloud, his voice echoing from the high canyon walls, from his favorite book: Sir Walter Scott's *The Lady of the Lake*.

Beaman, whose experience included piloting a ship on the Great Lakes, was assigned to pilot the third boat. Diaries from the expedition indicate that Powell frequently upbraided him for ignoring the hand signals.

Nonetheless, the boats made a safe journey from the Green River down to its junction with the Colorado. Powell frequently left the expedition to arrange for shipment of more supplies and to do mapping on his own.

Beaman reported to Anthony: "We have found our finest scenery in the roughest canyons; and here, while making from 10 to 15 portages in a day and running as many rapids at a breakneck speed, I have made from ten to twenty negatives." Beaman experienced frequent problems with the water in the area, which had a high mineral content, and often stained his plates. Windy conditions blew sand and dust onto the sticky collodion plates, and his portable dark-tent often blew down. "We often have to station a man at the tripod to keep the camera from going down the canyons on an exploring trip of its own," Beaman wrote. He frequently climbed the sides of the canyons to take pictures from the vantage points above.

The party was afflicted by illness and fatigue. Wolves harassed their camp, stealing a side of beef, leather, and anything containing grease. One night a wolf stole a ham from under the pillow of one of the party. By the end of December, the first year's expedition came to a halt and the party established a camp near Kanab, Utah.

Some members of the expedition had had enough of the river, including Beaman, who quit in January, 1872. He continued exploring on his own, taking two mules with his equipment to the Arizona desert, where he photographed ancient Aztec towns and the Indians who were still living there.

Powell took the 400 glass plates that Beaman had made to C. R. Savage's studio in Salt Lake City to have prints made. While there, he persuaded Savage's young assistant, James Fennemore, to accompany the survey party the following year.

104

Seventy years later, Fennemore racked his memory for the details of the expedition. He wrote: "It is impossible to go into the details of the almost hair-raising dangers of some of those rapids, in trying to run them with the boats—or making portages along the shores, at times up to our necks in water, carrying the provisions and bedding, and letting the boats through with ropes."

At one point, Powell led the men overland to map the surrounding country. They moved along the rim of the Grand Canyon in a blinding snowstorm, with Fennemore and his assistant Jack Hillers taking pictures under almost unbelievable conditions. When the weather cleared, Fennemore and Hillers carried the camera, plates, and chemicals down the face of the canyon wall. They clambered down about 2,500 feet, making their way over jagged rocks until they found a ledge to set the camera and dark-tent on. They made several pictures of the hundred-mile panorama that was spread out before them.

The party was plagued by hostile Indians and hordes of mosquitoes, and finally returned to Kanab to plan a new assault on the river. Fennemore resigned his post, leaving the task of photographing to John K. Hillers.

At the beginning of the trip, Hillers was an army veteran without education, working as a mule driver. Legend has it that he was out of work and staying in a Salt Lake City hotel when he overheard the Major's group in the next room drawing up plans for the trip downriver. He knocked on the door and volunteered. Though he may have been uneducated, Hillers proved a quick learner. After watching Beaman and serving as Fennemore's assistant, he was ready to serve as the full-fledged photographer of the expedition, a position he would hold for the next seven years.

The Major led six other men, including Hillers, in two boats into Marble Canyon on August 17, 1872. As the party moved downriver, the walls of the canyons became ever higher, reaching 6,000 feet above the water. Rapids became more treacherous, and often the current took the boats careening wildly down the river. The men were so soaked by the chilled water that they abandoned clothes altogether. They climbed the canyon walls to pluck fruit from cactuses growing in crevices to supplement their dwindling rations.

Many times, the sheer walls of the canyon came right up to the edge of the water so that there was no place to beach or portage the boats. They had to ride the rapids until a sand bar or tiny strip of shoreline appeared.

When a suitable spot for camp appeared, the men beached the boats, set up camp, and flopped exhausted on the rubber blankets they had brought. All but Hillers. He later recalled:

During the day, I would take my pictures, and when the night came and the boats were tied at the river bank, I would get out my darkroom and chemicals and develop the plates. Sometimes there would be enough light from a wood fire reflected down to the water to permit me to work. When there was no place to build a fire, someone would hold a lantern back of the light opening [in the portable dark-tent was a red window that allowed the worker to see dimly without spoiling his plates], and I would poke my head under the canvas and get to work. I missed a lot of sleep this way. When the water in the Colorado was muddy, we would watch for a clear stream emptying into the river and get a few bottles of fresh water for some of the finer work.

Powell's party reached the Little Colorado, the beginning of the Grand Canyon, on August 22. After this point, no landing place at all could be found, and at night the boats were tied to cliffs while the men slept in the boats or on overhanging ledges.

On September 3, one of the boats overturned in the rapids. Jack Hillers landed in a whirlpool and was sucked under. He escaped without his shoes and socks, which had been torn off by the whirling water. The Major, trying to pull men from the river into the second boat, slipped and fell into the whirlpool himself. Hillers jumped back in to save him.

JOHN K. HILLERS: Hillers at work with his glass plates in Powell's camp on the Aquarius Plateau, Utah Territory, in 1875. Some idea of the difficulty of transporting the photographer's equipment can be gotten from this view of the chemicals and apparatus around Hillers. On a tripod and covered with a dark-cloth is one of the mammoth cameras used by the survey photographers. Library of Congress

106

JOHN K. HILLERS: *The Zuñi pueblo, New Mexico, around 1879. This famous Indian community was discovered by the Spanish in 1539. Hillers made an extensive photographic study of the inhabitants and their culture, which still is practiced in some form by inhabitants of Zuñi today.* U.S. Geological Survey

Finally, on September 7, the party reached Kanab Canyon, where a supply party was waiting for them. On hearing that the Shivwit Indians, who had killed the three members of his earlier expedition, were again on the warpath, Powell called a halt to that season's work. The group went overland back to their base at Kanab, Utah.

Powell's survey continued until Congress consolidated the surveys into the U.S. Geological Survey in 1879. Hillers was with Powell every year. The Major was concerned with recording the culture of the Indians in the West, which he rightly feared would be destroyed by the coming of white settlement. Hillers's pictures of the Paiute, Ute, and Shoshone Indians are among the first ever taken of those tribes. The Utes gave him the name of "Myself-in-the-water," referring to the reflection of the photograph.

Hillers's Indian photographs, said by a modern critic to be "every bit as good as modern professional photography" and to "put to shame the efforts of most ethnologists," formed the basis of the collection of the Bureau of American Ethnology. Powell was first director of the Bureau. He supervised the recording of the way of life of the Indians of the West. Hillers, as his chief assistant, made more than 20,000 Indian photographs, both in the field and in the Washington studio of the Bureau.

Never again did Hillers meet the hardship and adventure of that trip down the Colorado. He wrote to the Major about the early photographs of that trip, saying he "was pleased with a good many, but some are not up to the mark. . . . I think we done middling for greenhorns." The wonder is that any pictures at all could have been taken under such conditions.

4

By 1871, Timothy O'Sullivan had returned from the Isthmus of Panama, where he had photographed the natives and the jungles for the Darien survey. By now, O'Sullivan's reputation as an experienced survey photographer was well known, and he was asked to participate in the army's own survey of the West, led by Lt. George M. Wheeler.

Wheeler had graduated from West Point in 1866, too late to make his army career in the Civil War. After the war, the size of the army was cut back, and the usual career for a military man was the lonely, hazardous life of the western soldier, holding isolated forts. Wheeler was assigned to be an engineer on the staff of the Commanding General of the Department of California. In this post, he explored Nevada and parts of Utah. His work earned him command of the new survey.

In establishing the Wheeler survey, the army's purpose was not a scientific one, although scientists accompanied the expedition and made important contributions. Wheeler's job was to make maps stressing human developments—mines, farms, villages, roads, railroads, dams . . . to give "a thorough knowledge of the conformation, the obstacles and resources of the country."

On the first year's survey, as well as in the years 1873 and 1875 when he also worked with Wheeler, O'Sullivan took many photographs of the Indians who inhabited the area, including Mojaves, Zuñis, Navajos, and Coyotero Apaches in Arizona, and the Utes and Jacarilla Apaches in New Mexico. Many of these were still hostile, and the Wheeler party was in frequent danger.

The men with Wheeler suffered other hardships. Rattlesnakes and poisonous centipedes plagued the group, and the blazing heat and long marches took their toll on expedition members. O'Sullivan seems to have borne the hardships well, for Wheeler frequently assigned him to command small parties that broke off from the main group.

Wheeler was a hard-driving officer, and he ran the survey as if he were fighting a desperate battle. The first year alone, Wheeler's men covered 72,250 square miles in Nevada, California, Utah, and Arizona. By Wheeler's own account, he kept the group on marches up to eighty hours long with scarcely a halt. On one day-long march, the group crossed Death Valley *at midday*, when the heat was so intense that O'Sullivan's photographic chemicals boiled.

Wheeler's temper was monumental, and his discipline seems to have been tinged with cruelty. He was accused of torturing Indian guides who failed to follow orders. Several men died under unexplained circumstances.

Wheeler's obstinacy is amply demonstrated by his decision in the first year of the survey to row, tow, or push three flat-bottomed boats *up* the Colorado River, against the rapids, from the California border to the Grand Canyon, a distance of 200 miles. There seems to have been no good reason for this trip, except as Wheeler described it—to determine the limits of practical navigation. Thirty-five men started out, with O'Sullivan in command of a boat he christened the *Picture.*

Each boat had six long oars, but they were all but useless. Most of the trip was made by men towing the boats through shallow water or struggling to carry them along the banks. The current was so strong that the boats themselves were an impediment, one more piece of baggage to be carried through the rattlesnake-infested canyons.

One boat was wrecked with the loss of Wheeler's reports,

instruments, and a supply of rations. The other boats, hammered against the sharp rocks of the river, began to leak badly. Wheeler pushed his group onward to his goal. It took 33 days of agonized labor for the group to travel the 200 miles upstream. Fifteen men of the original 35 deserted, drowned, or were left behind. The return journey, traveling with the current, took only five days.

Somehow, O'Sullivan saved his camera and plates and even managed to make pictures along the way. It was a terrible loss when the majority of his plates were lost in transit on a train back to Washington, D.C.

After the first year, Wheeler expanded the scope of his survey, planning a general mapping of United States territory west of the 100th meridian. William Bell, a Philadelphia photographer (not the same William Bell of the railroad surveys), accompanied Wheeler in 1872. His dispatches to a photographic magazine tell of some of the hardships of the work. He had to rise at 4 A.M. to load the mule carrying the photographic equipment. During the day, he had to stop and unload the mule whenever he wanted to make a picture. He reported a great deal of difficulty in keeping the plates sticky long enough to get a suitable exposure; perhaps this was because he lacked O'Sullivan's experience in taking pictures under these conditions. Bell was also plagued with wind blowing fine white alkali dust onto the sticky collodion.

Wheeler was not about to slow his march for the safety of a photographer who seemed incompetent anyway, and when Bell finished his photographing he had to repack the mule and try to catch up with the main party. By the time nightfall came, Bell was usually eight to ten miles behind the group. Finally arriving in camp, he had to water, unsaddle, and feed his mules and then find out if anyone had thought to save supper for him. Finally, he wrote, "If it is not one's turn on guard, [we] make our bed and retire, with our loaded carbine and pistol handy." One year of Wheeler's survey was enough for Bell.

In 1873 and 1875, O'Sullivan, now acting as Wheeler's "civilian assistant," led parties through the territory occupied by the Southwest Indian tribes. He photographed the city of Santa Fe, and he took a series of photographs that some regard as the culmination of his brilliant career.

In the Canyon de Chelly in Northern Arizona, O'Sullivan came upon the ruins of cliff-dwelling Indian tribes nestled against spectacular rock formations. Any photographer could make handsome pictures in such a setting, but O'Sullivan's views managed to capture the feeling of timeless grandeur and the ghostly presence of the long-dead race that built the pueblos.

In 1875, Wheeler bound prints of O'Sullivan's pictures into books containing the reports of the survey. Rather than have lithographers make copies of O'Sullivan's views that could be mechanically reproduced, Wheeler used the actual photographic prints. He required O'Sullivan to make 2,500 prints by hand—a forced march comparable to those he had led in the field.

O'Sullivan also made stereo cards of his prints, but these were not widely distributed. After 1875, O'Sullivan came east where he was the first photographer for the consolidated United States Geological Survey, which had Clarence King as its first director. If O'Sullivan took additional photographs in the period 1875–80, they have not survived.

In 1880, O'Sullivan obtained the post of photographer in the Treasury Department, but had to resign because of illness less than a year later. Suffering from tuberculosis, worn out from his years of work in the wilderness, O'Sullivan went home to his father's house on Staten Island, where he died in January, 1882, at the age of forty-two.

TIMOTHY H. O'SULLIVAN: The ruins in the Canyon de Chelly as photographed on the Wheeler expedition of 1873. National Archives

4

PHOTOGRAPHING THE INDIANS AND THE SOLDIERS

Photographs of the Indians taken for the surveys were made for ethnological purposes—to make a record of the culture of the people. Men like Powell and Hayden realized that as the Indians' culture became more and more affected by exposure to the settlers, soldiers, and explorers themselves, it would become diluted and lose its value for scientific study.

Photographs of Indians also appealed to a curious public, from the time when daguerreotypes of "Indian warriors" were appealing subjects in daguerrean galleries. Attitudes toward the Indians ranged from the view of them as "noble savages" to the opinion that they must be exterminated as quickly as possible to make the West safe for settlement and exploitation. Yet there was a universal fascination with views showing the reality of this "other" people who inhabited the continent.

Most interesting to the public were the Indians who actively fought the soldiers in a vain attempt to keep the land that had been ceded to them by the U.S. Government. Working near army posts such as Ft. Abraham Lincoln and Ft. Keogh, a series of photographers made a record of the Indians who resisted subjugation from just after the Civil War to 1890. Their views of the Plains Indians, chiefly Sioux and Comanche, helped create the image of an Indian in a long headdress, made so familiar later by Hollywood films. Studio photographers went so far as to keep on hand what was regarded as "typical" Indian dress to supply to Indians who might otherwise come to be photographed in nondescript, more practical attire.

In the early years of the nineteenth century, the Indian policy of the U.S. Government was relocation beyond the Mississippi. But with the opening of the Oregon Trail and the Santa Fe Trail to the far west, white settlers began to cross through Indian territory, an incursion deeply resented and feared by the Indians. To protect the white settlers, army posts were set up along the trails, further angering the Indians.

During the Civil War, the army withdrew many of its soldiers from frontier garrisons to serve in the War between the States. As a result, some of the Indians of the West went on the warpath. The worst of these wartime uprisings was among the Santee tribe in Minnesota in 1862.

As it happened, a photographer arrived in the area of the Minnesota Massacre just the day before the Indians attacked. Instead of taking pictures of peaceful Indians at work, Joel E. Whitney found himself fleeing to safety with a group of white refugees. He took a memorable photograph of them with his twin-lens stereo camera. After a detachment of troops arrived and put down the uprising, Whitney photographed the captured Indians. He sold his stereo views of the "Minnesota Massacre" from his gallery in St. Paul to a curious and horrified public. Whitney's views were. widely commented on in eastern newspapers and magazines.

After the Civil War, the Army turned full-time to the task of protecting settlers and railroad builders from the Indians. General William T. Sherman was appointed commander of the army in the West. His strategy was to construct a new line of forts for 600 miles along a band of territory that would be reserved for use of the whites. In addition, a line of three forts would be constructed on a road leading from Ft. Laramie on the Platte River north to gold fields around Virginia City, Montana.

One of the first Indian photographers after the war, Ridgway Glover, traveled to Ft. Laramie around the beginning of June, 1866. Glover was a correspondent for *Leslie's Illustrated Weekly* and the *Philadelphia Photographer*, to which he sent dispatches recounting his trip. In his first letter, he reported having some initial difficulty taking photographs of Indians at the fort, but after learning how to talk to them, he had more success. His chief complaint was the muddy water, which ruined over half the pictures he took.

Glover was described in the *Philadelphia Photographer* as "a rough, shaggy-looking fellow . . . he was a man of some means but loving the photographic art, took it up and became a very successful animal

JOEL E. WHITNEY: *The band of refugees from the Minnesota Massacre that Whitney traveled with, as they stopped for a rest.* Library of Congress

and landscape photographer. He was rather eccentric in his ways. We have often been amused at his odd-looking wagon as it passed our office window, and as frequently wondered that he secured as good results as he did. But he had his own way of thinking, and cared very little whether anyone else agreed with him or not."

Glover rode out to the Indians' camp near the fort. They had assembled in force for a parley with Col. Henry B. Carrington, who was attempting to sign a treaty with the Arapahoes, Cheyennes, and Sioux who had been raiding in Wyoming, Colorado, and Nebraska since 1864. Glover climbed a hill overlooking the camp, which he reported as having 200 lodges and 500 ponies, and attempted a picture.

When Glover rode into the camp itself, he found the Indians resistant to having their pictures taken. They "think photography is *pazuta zupa* (bad medicine)" he wrote. "Some of the Indians think they will die in three days, if they get their picture taken. At the ferry today I pointed the instrument at one of that opinion. The poor fellow fell on the sand, and rolled himself in his blanket."

Glover demonstrated with mirrors, and by showing the image on the ground glass screen of his camera, that "the light comes from the sun, strikes them, and then goes into the machine." He also gave the Indians ferrotypes, a type of inexpensive photograph made on black-enameled tin sheets, "and they think they are *wash-ta-le-poka* (Their superlative for good.)"

Carrington persuaded some of the chiefs to sign the treaty, but one of the chieftains, Red Cloud, stalked out of the negotiations, and the situation was still tense. Carrington left the fort with a party of 700 men, bound for Bozeman, Montana, to secure the road north. Glover went along.

At Ft. Reno, the first stop on the trail, Carrington found that Red Cloud's forces had attacked a wagon train and captured most of the horses and mules at Ft. Reno itself. Red Cloud sent a message to Carrington, warning him to return to Powder River.

But Carrington pressed onward, dispatching some men to begin construction of two more forts: Ft. Phil Kearny, at the Little Piney Fork, and Ft. C. F. Smith. Glover's next dispatch to the *Philadelphia Photographer* was dated July 29 from Ft. Phil Kearny. He recalled the sight at Ft. Laramie, where "I . . . saw the lazy, sleepy red man treating for peace and friendship. He has since appeared to me as the active, wide-awake savage on the warpath." Red Cloud's strategy was a kind of guerrilla warfare, attacking small groups of soldiers, and avoiding a major attack on the forts. Glover was with a group of sixteen soldiers, nine drivers, and ten civilians when it was attacked. The soldiers, armed with rifles, held the Indians off until a larger group of soldiers arrived. "They looked very wild and savage-like while galloping around us," Glover reported, "and I desired to make some instantaneous views, but our commander ordered me not to, as he expected an attack at any time." Farther on, another group of Cheyennes attacked the group's camp, but Glover was unable to prepare his plates for a photograph because his collodion was too hot.

Finally reaching Ft. Phil Kearny, Glover reported, "I am surrounded by beautiful scenery, and hemmed in by yelling savages, who are surprising and killing some one every day. I expect to get some good pictures here."

In one of his dispatches from Ft. Phil Kearny, Glover wrote, "Last week I took two days rations, and climbed the mountain just after sunrise." Later he went hunting game. His descriptions of the wilderness are rhapsodic, but he ignored the danger of Red Cloud's band. On September 14, Glover left the fort with one other man to take more views of the scenery. The *Philadelphia Photographer* reported, "It was known that the hostile Sioux were lurking around, but, knowing no fear, and being ardent in the pursuit of his beloved profession, he risked everything, and alas! the result was that he was scalped, killed, and horribly mutilated." Unfortunately, none of Glover's photographs are known to exist today.

Red Cloud's resistance continued through 1866 and into 1867. Finally, the government offered peace terms. Red Cloud, who had lost many warriors in the fighting, agreed to a parley. The government sent General Sherman with several Peace Commissioners to Ft. Laramie in April, 1868, to negotiate a treaty. A photographer was on hand to record the treaty negotiations. It may have been Alexander Gardner, who was at that time taking pictures of the railroad and surrounding towns in Kansas, and may have journeyed north for the council. Putting his name to the treaty as a witness was a photographer named George B. Withs, and it may have been he who took the pictures of the council and the Crow, Cheyenne, Arapahoe, and Sioux chiefs who attended.

121

Red Cloud himself stayed away from the council, and on another occasion is reported to have chased away a photographer who tried to take his picture. He was finally captured—on film—in 1870, when he visited Washington, D.C. The photographer was A. Zeno Schindler. Schindler ran a Washington gallery, and was one of many photographers who contributed photographs to a collection of Indian pictures made by an Englishman named William Blackmore. Blackmore's collection is today one of the most valuable archives of portraits of the Indians. He sent men all over the West to

ALEXANDER GARDNER or GEORGE B. WITHS: The U.S. Peace Commissioners and chiefs of the Sioux at Ft. Laramie in 1868. General Sherman is the third man from the left inside the lodge. National Archives

A. ZENO SCHINDLER: Red Cloud with William Blackmore in Schindler's Washington gallery. The Smithsonian Institution

obtain views for him. Later, Blackmore's collection went to the Bureau of American Ethnology at the Smithsonian Institution.

Other Washington, D.C., photographers, notably Mathew Brady and Alexander Gardner, also made photographs of the Indians who were invited there to meet the "Great Father" (the President) and his officials. For some of these pictures, the Indians were "dressed up" to fit the public image of what an Indian should look like. The chiefs often arrived in odds and ends of white man's clothing, rather than their traditional dress, and the gallery owners maintained a collection of Indian "costumes" for the portraits. Mrs. Gardner, for one, complained of the "smelly collection" of feathers and beads and hides that was kept in the gallery.

William Stinson Soule was a photographer who lived in the Indian territory for eight years. He left as full a record as we are likely to have of the way Indians looked when they were still unsubdued by the white culture. Soule lived on army posts in the Indian territory of the southern Plains during the time when General Philip Sheridan was waging his campaign against the Kiowa, Comanche, Arapahoe, and Cheyenne tribes.

As an army post photographer, Soule made his living chiefly by taking portraits for the officers and men to send to their loved ones back home. The Soule photographs that remain show what life was like on a military post in the West just after the Civil War.

Soule had been born in Maine in 1836 and served with the Union forces during the war. He had been wounded at Antietam. After the war he worked in a photographic gallery in Chambersburg, Pennsylvania.

Sometime in early 1867 Soule brought his photographic gear to Ft. Dodge, Kansas. The first published record of his work was an engraving made from one of his photographs in *Harper's Weekly* in January, 1869. The picture shows a sheepherder lying dead and scalped near Ft. Dodge. Illustrations of such savagery were used to fan public sentiment against the Indians of the Plains.

In late 1868 or early 1869 Soule went to Camp Supply in the Indian territory, which Sheridan was establishing as a base of operations. What little we know of Soule's career comes from the photographic record. He documented the construction of Ft. Sill early in 1870, and probably opened a photographic gallery there. Indians came to the

WILLIAM S. SOULE: An Arapaho camp near Ft. Dodge, Kansas. Buffalo meat is being dried on the wooden frame behind the Indians in foreground. National Archives

fort as prisoners and for treaty parleys, and Soule was able to make a record of a great many of them. These were Indians who had killed white soldiers and settlers, and were engaged in an active struggle with the United States Army. In the East Soule's photographs attracted the attention of a public curious to see what these warriors actually looked like.

Soule left Ft. Sill in late 1874 or early 1875 and returned to Boston. His brother John had copyrighted many of his photographs for sale by the family business. William Soule set up a studio in Boston, which he operated until 1902. He died in 1908.

One of the great legendary figures of the American West was George A. Custer, given the courtesy title of "General" because of his temporary generalship in the Civil War. Custer aspired to higher office than another generalship, and he showed a fondness for photographers and the publicity they could bring. Custer was active in the campaign on the southern Plains with Sheridan, but if Soule photographed him the picture does not survive.

Placed in command of Ft. Abraham Lincoln, near Bismarck in the Dakota Territory, after the southern Plains Indians had been subdued, Custer embarked on the campaign against the Sioux and related tribes that would bring him to an end different from the one he had hoped for.

The northern Plains tribes were again on the warpath. White settlers and prospectors, and surveyors for the northern railroads, had violated the treaty of Ft. Laramie, and the Indians saw more and more whites invading the land ceded to them by treaty.

In 1873, Custer and his Seventh Cavalry accompanied an expedition to the Yellowstone led by General David Stanley to lay out a possible route for the Northern Pacific Railroad. Official photographer for the party was William R. Pywell, who had been one of Brady's photographers during the war. His services were considered so valuable that Stanley's survey allotted the sum of one thousand dollars for photographic apparatus and material.

Unfortunately, bureaucratic fumbling resulted in Pywell's photographic wagon and equipment being sent by boat directly to the Yellowstone, while the survey party journeyed from Ft. Rice by horse and wagon. It was not till almost a month later that the frustrated Pywell caught up with his equipment and began taking pictures. Nonetheless, he took at least a hundred stereo views and nine 11″ × 14″ prints of the Yellowstone, which he offered from his Washington gallery the following year. The most famous of these pictures shows Custer, in buckskin suit and long golden hair, with an elk he had shot.

In 1874 Custer led an expedition through the Black Hills area of the Dakota Territory, ostensibly to find a site for a fort, but also to learn if gold was to be found in the area.

The Black Hills area held a religious significance for the Plains Indians, and they had been ceded full control of it by the treaty of 1868. Nonetheless, prospectors had been coming to the area to search for the gold that was reputedly there, and soon the Northern Pacific Railroad would be building its tracks through. Custer expected to meet with a hostile force of Sitting Bull's men, and he prepared a large, well-armed expedition.

WILLIAM R. PYWELL: Lt. Col. George A. Custer posing with an elk he has shot on the survey party led by General David S. Stanley in 1873. The buckskin outfit was Custer's customary attire while campaigning; he was wearing one like it on his fatal mission at the Little Big Horn. National Park Service, Department of Interior. Custer Battlefield National Monument

Custer had approximately 1,000 men and 1,000 horses with 110 wagons, each drawn by 6 mules, and a herd of 300 cattle for provisions. The expedition made an impressive sight strung out along the beautiful valleys in the region, and fortunately there was a photographer along to make a record.

William H. Illingworth emigrated with his family from Great Britain and arrived in St. Paul, Minnesota, in 1850, when he was a boy of eight. He learned photography as an apprentice in Chicago, and by the time he was twenty-two, he was listed as a photographer in the St. Paul City Directory.

In 1866, Illingworth and his partner, George Bill, had traveled with the expedition of Capt. James L. Fisk to Montana to map a safe road for whites trying to reach the Montana gold fields overland. The two photographers produced about thirty stereo views of military posts and Indian camps along the route. They stopped at Fort Union, at the junction of the Yellowstone and Missouri rivers, and took the only known photographs of the fort, which was destroyed the following year. Illingworth and Bill's stereo views of the expedition sold well. When Bill quit the business, the Fisk negatives were sold to John Carbutt, who sold stereo views made from them under his own name.

Illingworth continued to operate a successful gallery in St. Paul. He took hundreds of stereographs of Minnesota scenery and issued them as stereos. When the opportunity came to travel with Custer's expedition, and to keep the negatives for his growing stereo business, he accepted eagerly. Illingworth traveled to Ft. Abraham Lincoln in time to leave with the expedition on July 2.

At times, Illingworth apparently traveled far in advance of the expedition to allow himself time to transport his portable darkroom to the top of a hill or bluff, prepare his plates, and be ready to photograph the wagons as they streamed by hundreds of feet below. His courage in traveling alone, when rumors at the fort had said that 5,000 Sioux lay in wait for them, must have impressed Custer. Custer named one of the valleys they mapped "Illingworth Valley."

The party encountered only a few small groups of Indians, but found a little gold and much in the way of beautiful scenery for Illingworth's camera. At one point, the party followed Spring Creek through a valley that had multitudes of flowers growing in it. Custer himself wrote:

In no private or public park have I ever seen such a profuse display of flowers . . . men plucked them without dismounting from the saddle. . . . It was a strange sight to glance back at the advancing columns of cavalry and behold the men with beautiful bouquets in their hands, while the headgear of the horses was decorated with wreaths of flowers fit to crown a queen of the May.

The party camped on the spot, and it was a perfect idyll, with a military band serenading the men as they ate.

On July 30 the party established camp at a site which later became Custer City. The following year would find it a growing mining city of 11,000 people.

Custer arrived back at Ft. Abraham Lincoln on August 30, having traveled 883 miles in 60 days. Custer's report, which described the area as having "gold from the grassroots down," would bring an influx of prospectors into the hills.

Illingworth, back in St. Paul, was arguing with the government over possession of his negatives. He finally won out, but the market for stereos was in a slump, and his business suffered. Illingworth showed a weakness for drink. His wife, citing his bouts of drunkenness and his cruelty toward her, divorced him, a most unusual action at the time. Finally, impoverished and alone, Illingworth shot himself in 1893, leaving behind almost nothing but his collection of 1,600 negatives, a priceless heritage.

There were others who fared better. One, Stanley J. Morrow, would have achieved a measure of fame if only for the fact that he passed up a chance to become the official photographer at Custer's Last Stand.

Morrow was born in Ohio in 1843, and moved to Wisconsin around 1860. He served as a private in the Civil War, with the Army of the Potomac. In 1864 he served at Point Lookout Prison in Maryland where, tradition holds, he learned photography from Mathew Brady. When Morrow returned to Wisconsin and married in December, 1865, his profession was "photographist."

In the fall of 1868 Morrow and his wife, Isa, traveled by covered wagon to Yankton in the Dakota Territory, where they established a gallery. During most summers, Morrow's habit was to outfit a wagon with photographic equipment and make long journeys as far as the Yellowstone region. Considering the danger during much of this period with the Indian wars going on, Morrow's journeys are remarkable. He photographed army posts, Indian agencies, and warriors and chiefs of many tribes, including the Sioux, Cheyennes, Bannocks, Asiniboins, and Crows.

Though he seems to have established a rapport with the Indians, Morrow was in danger several times. On one trip, he was attempting to photograph the unusual Sioux method of entombing their dead by placing them in coffins atop scaffolds. An Indian guard threatened Morrow with his rifle, and Morrow began to back gingerly away. He reached into his back pocket, where he carried nothing but a corkscrew and a pocket knife. He clicked the two together, making the Indian think he was cocking a revolver, and Morrow managed to withdraw safely.

Morrow's wife, who sometimes accompanied him on these trips, reported that they were holed up in a ranchhouse for several days, while hostile Indians surrounded the place threatening attack. Nevertheless, in the summer of 1873, Morrow felt such confidence in his relationship with the Indians that he took both his wife and daughter with him on a trip to Montana.

In November, 1871, Morrow hired Orlando Scott Goff to come to Yankton to operate the gallery in Morrow's frequent absences. Goff, then twenty-eight years old, had worked in a photographic studio, possibly Morrow's, in Portage, Wisconsin. He would soon make a reputation of his own, and in 1873 was in business with a partner at Ft. Abraham Lincoln. Like Morrow, he traveled widely to make stereo views, journeying into the Upper Missouri and Yellowstone valleys to photograph the army forts there.

Goff took many pictures of George Custer and the officers and men of the Seventh Cavalry at Ft. Abraham Lincoln. When Goff married in 1875, he and his wife entered into the social life of the military garrison, of which Mrs. Custer was the leader. Goff's pictures of life at the fort show an active community and avoid the stilted studio shots taken by other post photographers.

The winter of 1875–76 brought matters between the army and Sitting Bull's Sioux to a head. The government's offer to "lease" the

Black Hills had been rejected, and the army announced that any Indian who failed to report to the reservation by January 31, 1876, would be considered "hostile." General George Crook had been placed in charge of the region to enforce the order. In April Sitting Bull held council with the chiefs of the Sioux, the Cheyennes, and the Arapahoes. They decided to fight.

In May General Alfred H. Terry, with a thousand men including Custer's Seventh Cavalry, departed from Ft. Abraham Lincoln. They were to link up with similarly large forces under General Crook and General John Gibbon to defeat the northern tribes once and for all.

Morrow, at Ft. Abraham Lincoln, had received permission to accompany Custer, but a supply of needed chemicals failed to arrive from Chicago in time. Morrow was left frustrated at the fort, not knowing what a lucky man he was.

Custer, eager to make a spectacular victory, led a 211-man command against a massive force of 2,500 warriors led by Chiefs Gall and Crazy Horse. On June 25, 1876, on the Little Big Horn River, Custer's troopers were wiped out to the last man.

Crook and Terry followed the Indians all summer, looking for another battle. But the Indians split up and eluded them. Crazy Horse and his band turned back toward the Black Hills, and Crook's men followed. The soldiers began to run out of food, and many of the men broke down from sheer exhaustion. Crook drove his forces ever harder, trying to catch up with Crazy Horse. In September Crook sent 150 men with the best horses—some of the weakest horses had been used for food—to the Black Hills settlements for supplies.

Morrow was in Deadwood, awaiting news. When Crook's advance force staggered in, Morrow accompanied the supply party to photograph what later became known as the "Horse Meat March."

At the news of Custer's death, the nation demanded revenge, and a massive military force spent the winter isolating Crazy Horse and his warriors in an attempt to starve them into submission. In December, at the Red Cloud agency, Morrow photographed the ceremonies as General Crook made Spotted Tail the chief of the Sioux.

At the installation of Spotted Tail, old Chief Red Cloud was brought in as a prisoner. Morrow wrote, "Through the kindness of the Indian trader, Mr. Dear, I was enabled to procure some good negatives of Red Cloud today, it being the first time he ever gave a sitting to a photographer." Morrow evidently didn't know of Red Cloud's earlier sitting for Schindler.

Spotted Tail and his men, many of whom Morrow also photographed, assisted the government in defeating Crazy Horse, who surrendered the following spring. Morrow's photograph of Crazy-in-the-Lodge, the head warrior under Spotted Tail, has sometimes been incorrectly identified as Crazy Horse. Crazy Horse, almost

STANLEY J. MORROW: An incident on General Crook's "Horse Meat March" in pursuit of Crazy Horse in 1876. Though many of Morrow's photographs seem to have been "staged" for effect, the troopers were actually reduced to eating their own horses, and this one would seem to have needed to be put out of its misery in any case. W. H. Over Museum, University of South Dakota

alone among the major Indian leaders, always resisted capture by the "shadow-catchers." No authentic photograph of him is known to exist.

Farther west, Sitting Bull had fled into Canada, and the army established two new posts in the Yellowstone area—Ft. Keogh, at the mouth of the Tongue River, and Ft. Custer, at the junction of the Big Horn and Little Big Horn. Ft. Meade was established to protect mining operations in the Black Hills.

At Ft. Keogh, a man named John H. Fouch was official post photographer from May, 1877, to November, 1878. In June of 1877, a party of soldiers came to Ft. Keogh with orders to find and return with the bodies of Custer and his officers. For Fouch, who marketed stereo views "of the Yellowstone Country, Yellowstone National Park (and) Portraits of Celebrated Indian Chiefs," this was a magnificent opportunity. There would be an unprecedented demand for views of the battle site. But the officer in charge of the party refused to allow photographers or reporters to accompany his men.

Not long after, however, Philetus W. Norris, the new superintendent of Yellowstone National Park, passed through the fort. Norris was also a correspondent for a New York newspaper, and was using his position to try to get a scoop. He had no time to wait for Fouch, but on his return, gave Fouch directions to the battlefield and supplied him with provisions.

Fouch did market stereo views of the battle site, and it is possible they were taken that year. The following year, 1877, he also took a photograph of Chief Joseph of the Nez Percés, who had just been brought to Ft. Keogh after his surrender to General Nelson A. Miles.

When Fouch left, apparently for Minneapolis, where he operated a photographic gallery later, Morrow arrived on the scene at Ft. Keogh. In August, he had been appointed as post photographer at Ft. Custer, and now he received a similar appointment for Ft. Keogh, using the three-room, 18-by-40-foot cabin that had been Fouch's. By 1878, white settlers were arriving at the Yellowstone River country, and Ft. Keogh was on the regular mail routes to the West Coast. The Bannock Indians staged a short uprising, which General Miles put down, and Morrow photographed the captives at the stockade at Ft. Keogh.

The following year, Morrow accompanied the military detail that

133

was assigned to reburial duty at the Custer Battlefield to erect proper markers over the fallen men. This was the end of Morrow's photographing in the field. In December, 1879, he left Ft. Keogh and returned to Yankton, where he continued to operate his studio until retirement in 1883.

Morrow's successor at Ft. Keogh was Laton Alton Huffman, a young man of twenty-five. When Huffman was eleven, his father operated a photographic studio in Waukon, Iowa. Huffman learned his father's trade, but led a footloose early life. He spent his teenage years working as a wrangler on horseback, became a surveyor for the Northern Pacific Railroad, and in 1878 worked in the photographic studio of Frank Jay Haynes at Moorhead, Minnesota.

At Ft. Keogh, Huffman received no salary as post photographer. His income came from the sale of pictures. He also doubled as a guide for hunting parties, sold buffalo hides, and started a small cattle ranch.

Huffman's studio at the fort became a congenial gathering place for soldiers, scouts, and Indians who relished an hour or two of conversation with a drink and a cigar. "Yellowstone" Kelly, the famous trapper and scout, was a frequent visitor, as was Spotted Bear, an old chief of the Cheyennes.

In early 1880, General Miles's soldiers captured some of Sitting Bull's band who had been raiding on the American side of the border. Among those captured was Rain-in-the-Face, who was crippled at the Battle of the Little Big Horn, and was reputed to have killed General Custer at the battle. Huffman realized that a picture of him would be a big seller in his collection of views. However, General Miles put him in a prisoner-of-war camp just west of Ft. Keogh, and kept civilians away.

Huffman sneaked into the camp in a delivery wagon bearing provisions, and persuaded Rain-in-the-Face to join him for the trip back to the photographic studio at the post. He spent three hours photographing him in various regalia that were collected in the studio.

Rain-in-the-Face's band became agitated when his absence was discovered. Believing him to have been taken by the whites to be killed or sent away, they threatened violence. Huffman soon brought the chief back, but was then called to Miles's office.

Huffman wrote that Miles was obviously "hot around the collar." Miles told him, "Young man, if you ever take another prisoner out of camp without permission from the adjutant or myself, you will find yourself in very serious trouble." Huffman gave his word, glad to have gotten off so easily. He made a tidy profit from the sale of those pictures.

In 1881 Sitting Bull was persuaded to come back to the United States. His surrender took place at Ft. Buford, Dakota Territory, on July 19. It marked the end of the government's long conflict with the Indians of the Northern Plains.

Sitting Bull and his band of 187 men, women, and children boarded a steamboat to make the trip down the Missouri River to the Standing Rock Reservation. On August 1, the boat stopped at the town of Bismarck, where Orlando Goff had his studio. Goff asked to take the chief's picture.

At first Sitting Bull refused. He had never allowed his picture to be taken, and although his body was a captive, his spirit was still free. Finally Goff persuaded him to pose, saying later that the chief accepted an offer of $50. Sitting Bull allowed Goff to take but one, and then left the studio hastily.

Goff's picture shows a defeated yet still proud man, an Indian who had clung to the "wild" ways. Later Sitting Bull became a kind of "show" Indian, sitting for his portrait many times, even joining the Buffalo Bill Cody touring Wild West Show for a year. He became a national celebrity. Goff's picture of him, enlarged to many times its original size, was a popular exhibit at the Chicago World's Fair of 1893.

It was around 1878 that Goff took on an assistant, David F. Barry, then about twenty-five years old. Barry and his family had moved from New York State to Columbia County, Wisconsin, in the early 1860s. They stayed there until 1870, and it is quite possible that Barry as a boy knew Goff and Morrow, who were both working as photographers in the area. It may have been in one of their studios that he worked, as he later recalled, carrying water up several flights of stairs for darkroom use.

For a few years, Goff and Barry worked as an effective team. Goff was inclined to take his darkroom on wheels out into the wilder areas of the West to photograph Indians and garrison life. Goff left

135

his studio in Barry's charge in September, 1879, while Goff set out to spend the fall and winter with his photographic wagon around Ft. Meade. Later in the year, Barry extended the business, reopening the old studio at Ft. Abraham Lincoln to promote business from the soldiers stationed there. The following May, 1880, Barry himself set out for Ft. Buford, where he set up a mobile gallery and took pictures of the soldiers there.

The stories of the two photographers become tangled, because Barry later changed the details of his own autobiography to make it seem as if he had been responsible for all of Goff's pictures, including the early ones of Custer at Ft. Abraham Lincoln. By this time, Goff was dead, and Barry had bought his negatives, publishing them under his own name.

One story that Barry liked to tell concerned the time in early 1881 when he had finished his work at Ft. Buford and was on the road again when he heard that Sitting Bull and his band were being brought to the fort. He rushed back and obtained permission to photograph the Indians.

Barry was not as persuasive as his mentor, and could not get Sitting Bull to agree to being photographed. He did entice Chief Gall to the studio, and the conquerer of Custer appeared, according to Barry, "just as you would see him in camp." Gall would not sit down, and Barry took a standing pose of him.

Later, when Gall called to see his picture, Barry wrote,

he declared . . . that it was "bad" (ab-se-vah). I took the plate out of his hand . . . and placed it in my little darkroom. Gall then said that he wanted the picture to throw away [and] started to get it himself from the darkroom. I had to act quickly, so I gave him a push away from the door. As quick as a flash, Gall drew his knife, and I saw in an instant that he was furious. I took one step back into the darkroom and reached for my revolver on the shelf. I covered Gall, who with uplifted knife was almost

ORLANDO SCOTT GOFF: *Sitting Bull just after his surrender in 1881.* The Edward E. Ayer Collection, the Newberry Library, Chicago

upon me. Just one instant's terrible pause, and then Chief Gall stepped back [and] slowly backed out of my place.

Barry regaled many an audience with the story.

Goff sold his Bismarck gallery to Barry in 1884 and moved west, operating galleries at Ft. Custer, Ft. Assiniboine, and Havre, Montana. In the nineties, a fire burned his studio at Havre to the ground, consuming his collection of photographs, including the enlargement of Sitting Bull that had been exhibited at the Chicago World's Fair. In 1900, Goff finally retired, but continued to live in Montana and Idaho until his death in 1917.

Barry had duplicates of most of Goff's negatives in the Bismarck studio, and after 1886 began to market them along with his own fine collection of views. In 1890 he moved to Superior, Wisconsin, where he lived (with the exception of 1897, when he tried to operate a gallery in New York City for a year) until his death in 1934.

ORLANDO SCOTT GOFF: Sioux Indians being taken by riverboat to the Standing Rock Indian Reservation, near Bismarck, around 1880. State Historical Society of North Dakota

DAVID F. BARRY: Indian agents were supposed to distribute fresh meat to the Indians on reservations. Indians resisted the offers of slaughtered sides of beef, which often were spoiled and of inferior quality. They asked that the cattle be delivered live, and on the distribution date each Indian could pick out one for himself, shoot it, and take it home. It was a sad parody of the days when Indian hunters roamed the Plains, killing buffalo from horseback for food. Denver Public Library Western History Department

F. Jay Haynes, the Northern Pacific's photographer, took numerous pictures of the Indians along the railroad line. In 1881, he visited the Custer Battlefield site to photograph the monument that had just been erected. At the Crow reservation nearby, he "discovered" Curly, the Indian scout who had left Custer's troop just before the battle. Haynes's picture of him helped make Curly a western legend.

In 1885, Haynes also made photographs of the Flathead reservation in northwest Montana. His views were used by the government to show the success of the official policy of "civilizing" the Indians.

The Flatheads had accepted white ways, had a cattle ranch, a lumbermill, and a Catholic Church.

But a more tragic story is symbolized by the famous photograph of Chief Joseph of the Nez Percés that Haynes made in Bismarck in November, 1877. Joseph and his band were being moved from Ft. Keogh to a reservation in Indian Territory. The government was sending him and his people to a malaria-ridden reservation in a strange country far to the south instead of allowing them to live on their land in Idaho, as had been promised. At the time the photograph was taken, Joseph was still unaware of the government's treachery.

One photographer, because of his position as a soldier for the United States Army, had the opportunity to photograph the Indians on many of the fronts where they fought the white man. Christian Barthelmess came to the United States from Germany in the early 1870s to escape the universal conscription in his native country.

By 1876, Barthelmess had enlisted in the United States Army, destined to see service against the Indians, rather than the French. On his first enlistment, Barthelmess served in Arizona as part of the Sixth Cavalry protecting the scattered white settlements against Apaches. While in the area, Barthelmess, a well-read man for the time, became interested in ethnological studies of the Indians, and observed and photographed some of the ceremonies of the Navajos. He wrote articles on his experiences for *Der Western*, a German-language newspaper in Chicago.

In 1887 Barthelmess was transferred to Ft. Lewis in southwestern Colorado. Powell's expedition eight years earlier had brought prospectors and fortune-seekers to the Grand Canyon (450 miles from Ft. Lewis) and the upper Colorado River. Barthelmess accompanied an army expedition to the canyon during his stay.

In 1888, Barthelmess was sent to Ft. Keogh. There had been no post photographer since Huffman had moved to Miles City. Possibly with the encouragement of General Miles, who knew of Barthelmess's work, the soldier-photographer built a new darkroom and studio at the fort.

By this time, Barthelmess had married, and the social life of the fort in the late eighties and nineties became a subject for his camera. In 1890, he photographed the army Indian scouts who were training

140

FRANK J. HAYNES: *Chief Joseph of the Nez Percés. The Nez Percés, whose first encounter with white men dated to the Lewis and Clark expedition, boasted that they had always lived in peace. But when they resisted transportation to the reservation, they were attacked by U.S. cavalry. Joseph led his band on a long retreat, trying to escape into Canada, but finally surrendered when he was promised decent living conditions for the tribe, another promise quickly broken. The Nez Percés were later permitted to return to the Northwest.* **The Haynes Foundation**

at Ft. Keogh for action against the last-gasp remnant of the hostile Sioux in the Ghost Dance campaign.

Barthelmess retired from the army in 1903, but continued to serve as post photographer in a civilian capacity until his death in 1906. After his death, many of his negatives were sold to L. A. Huffman. They were incorporated into the Huffman collection and are among those views bearing Huffman's name today.

In the Southwest, the army was called on to defend settlers and prospectors against the various Apache tribes. A silver strike in the area around Tombstone, Arizona, in 1877, brought many prospectors to the region. Among those who came as tradespeople were Camillus S. Fly and his wife of two months, Mary E. Goodrich. Both

CAMILLUS S. FLY: Geronimo, on right, standing with his son and two braves at the 1886 conference with General Crook. Department of Library, Archives, and Public Records, State of Arizona

the Flys were capable photographers. Camillus Fly was then thirty years old. He and his wife built a rooming house and photographic gallery and were part of the life of the colorful and often violent community that called itself "the town too tough to die."

During the Flys' early years in Tombstone, a major fear of the residents was the Chiricahua Apache tribe which roamed through Mexico and the southwest United States in small bands. Victorio, Cochise, and Geronimo were some of their most famous leaders, and of these perhaps the most feared was Geronimo.

Geronimo's long-running battle with the governments of Mexico and the United States stemmed from an incident in 1858 when Mexican soldiers made an unprovoked attack on his village, killing his mother, wife, and children. From then on he waged a campaign

No. 174—Geronimo, Son and Two Picked Braves. Man with Lone Rifle Geronimo.

of attacking on one side of the international border, then fleeing to safety on the other side until the soldiers sent to capture him had given up.

Geronimo spent four years on the San Carlos Reservation between 1877 and 1881, but then broke out and began terrorizing the Southwest. He was brought back to the reservation several times between then and September, 1886, but he always escaped again.

In March, 1886, General George Crook succeeded through an emissary in persuading Geronimo to surrender. Crook was allowed by the Mexican government to meet with Geronimo in the Sierra Madre Mountains south of the international border. On this occasion Camillus Fly and an assistant named Chase went with Crook.

Fly succeeded in making a number of pictures of the camp of the hostile Apaches, as well as the conference between Geronimo and Crook. The pictures were reprinted in *Harper's Weekly*, giving Fly national fame for a time.

Unfortunately, the affair turned into something of a fiasco when Geronimo abruptly left the military party that was to bring him back to the United States. Crook lost his post, and General Nelson Miles had to recapture Geronimo in September of the same year. It is worth noting that at the time of his capture, Geronimo's band consisted of fewer than a hundred men, women, and children; yet he had managed to resist capture by 42 companies of U.S. cavalry and infantry as well as 4,000 Mexican soldiers.

Either Camillus or "Mollie" Fly wrote a description of Geronimo in their book of pictures of him and his people. Written twenty years after Geronimo had ceased to be a threat, it gives some idea of the hatred and fear that were felt toward him. He is described as:

a typical American Bedouin with his hand against everyman and every man's hand against him. He is, perhaps, the most conspicuous surviving instance of monumental villainy in existence. . . . Springing from an ancestry in the black ventricles of whose hearts the clotted ooze of robbery and murder was ever creeping, his subsequent record for sublime villainy is not surprising. . . .

Geronimo, who lived till 1909, when he was probably past ninety, became something of a celebrity. In the reservations in Florida and Ft. Sill, Oklahoma, he made a living selling photographs of himself

144

and bows and arrows with his name on them. When he visited the Smithsonian Institution in Washington, he charged 25¢ to the curator for his autograph and demanded another "two bits" for permission to take his photograph. "I had only 15 cents in change and my smallest bill was a dollar," recalled DeLancey Gill, the photographer at the Smithsonian, who had taken the portraits of many Indians. "So I borrowed a dime and gave Geronimo two dimes and a nickel. The wily old rascal palmed one of the dimes on me and held out 15 cents, crying, 'two bits! two bits!' So I had to change my dollar and give him another dime to get that photograph."

Other photographers in the Southwest befriended some of the tribes that were less hostile and made a record of their customs and life. One of these men was Charles F. Lummis, who had been a newspaper editor in Los Angeles before coming to New Mexico in 1888 for his health. He lived among the Pueblo Indians for a time, and devoted his later career to photographing and collecting artifacts of the Spanish, Mexican, and Indian cultures of the Southwest. Later he founded the Southwest Museum in Los Angeles with his collection.

Ben Wittick, who was born in 1845, had operated a portrait gallery in Moline, Illinois, after the Civil War. In 1878 he became a photographer for one of the railroads then building track through New Mexico. He started a gallery in Santa Fe in 1878, followed by a gallery in Albuquerque in partnership with R. W. Russell in 1883. Later, he had studios at Gallup and Ft. Wingate. He took some of the earliest pictures of the snake dance of the Hopi Indians, and photographed the Navajo chief, Manuelito. He photographed some of the chiefs and scenes of battles during the last Apache war. In 1903, Wittick died when he was bitten by a rattlesnake that he had collected for one of the Hopi rituals.

In 1883, Wittick took his son on a photographic trip to the Grand Canyon. The son wrote a long letter to his mother and brothers, who were still back in Moline, describing the trip. On their way back, the Witticks camped near a tribe of Walapai Indians, and the son wrote with feeling of their condition: "A good many of these Indians have died lately, of small-pox and starvation. . . . They were all near starving a short time ago. The government feeds and keeps the

Apache, . . . while these poor cusses, who have been faithful friends of the government for ten years, and fought Apaches, don't receive any notice."

Wittick and his son photographed the Indians with a stereo camera and a large 11" × 14" plate camera. The photographing made the Indians restless, and the son wrote, "They couldn't understand what that . . . meant . . . unless it was to make harm come to them, and give us a charm over them. One of them . . . came over to us and asked, 'All Injins die now? That make all Injins go dead, eh, bymebye, mebbe?' " The Witticks told the Indians they were Mormons, who were known to be friends, and the band was pacified.

The end of the Indian wars came with one last massacre. In 1890 a strange cult began to sweep through the Indian tribes of the

northern Plains. Pacified now and kept on reservations, the Indians had found that reservation life meant exposure to disease, poverty, and more parleys where the government would take more land. The Ghost Dance religion, as the cult was known, offered an appealing list of promises: the Indian dead would rise from their graves, the white men would go away, and life would be as it had been before. All that was necessary for these things to happen was that the Indians should dance the "Ghost Dance."

Though there was no threat to settlers or soldiers from the cult, the government became alarmed at the news that the Indians were spending much of their time dancing and praying for a Messiah to come. The cult was banned.

A group of Indians, led by Chief Big Foot, who were reputed to be ghost dancers, were thought to be dangerous. Soldiers were sent to

G. F. TRAGER: *The body of Big Foot, frozen in the snow at Wounded Knee.* National Archives

Settlement of the West: Forts, towns, sites of military engagements, and scenic points recorded by photographers.

capture them. In reality, Big Foot's band was struggling through the wintry plains toward the safety of the Pine Ridge Reservation. When the soldiers under Major Samuel Whitside of the Seventh Cavalry encountered them on December 28, 1890, the major decided to disarm the group. As soldiers searched their belongings, a shot rang out. Soldiers stationed around the camp with machine guns opened fire.

Between 150 and 300 of the original band of 350 men, women, and children were wiped out. Taking 50 wounded survivors back to the Pine Ridge Agency, Whitside awaited the end of a fierce blizzard to return to the spot, at Wounded Knee, where the massacre had taken place. When he returned, several photographers including G. F. Trager of Chadron, Nebraska, went along to photograph the frozen and contorted figures of the last Indians killed in a battle with the U.S. Army.

A correspondent for the Washington *Star* wrote about the photographers who had gathered at Pine Ridge to make pictures of the Ghost Dance "war":

Most particularly desirable . . . was the opportunity to photograph the battlefields while the dead were still lying thereon. Such chances are not numerous in this country and at this date. They are desirable for the money that is in them, when viewed from the photographic standpoint. . . .

It was hard work . . . to fill the orders that tumbled in from all parts of the country. When the battlegrounds and the earthworks and the buildings had been photographed, then commenced the lucre-catching job of making pictures of the army by companies. Of course, every soldier wanted all the scenes of the war and at least one copy of the photograph in which he was a figure. There was money in the business.

149

5

IMAGES OF
FRONTIER LIFE

When Camillus and "Mollie" Fly set up their boarding house and photographic studio in Tombstone, Arizona, in 1879, they hardly imagined that they would become part of one of the great legends of the West. But they had chosen a propitious spot—right in front of the entrance to the O.K. Corral.

Violence was rampant in Tombstone, marked by a long-standing feud between the townspeople and the cowboys and miners who lived outside the town. Even the lawmen were on opposing sides. Town Marshal Virgil Earp was often at odds with County Sheriff John Behan, whose constituency included the cowhands.

Matters came to a head on October 26, 1881, at what is remembered as the Gunfight at the O.K. Corral. Marshal Earp, his brothers Wyatt and Morgan, and Dr. John Holliday met four other men in deadly combat right alongside Fly's gallery. Sheriff Behan watched the fight from the safety of Fly's rooming house, and Ike Clanton, the only cowboy to survive, fled through Fly's house to escape.

When the shots died away, Fly himself appeared on the scene, not—to our great loss—with a camera, but a rifle. It must have seemed an occasion when the requirements of safety outweighed the demands of history.

The town saloon keeper testified at the trial that followed: "I saw Fly come out of his house with a Henry rifle in his hand. He made a remark about Billy Clanton who was lying on his back with a pistol in his right hand. 'Somebody take that pistol away from that man,' he said. I said to Mr. Fly, 'Go and get it yourself if you want it.'

"Billy Clanton," the saloon keeper recalled, "seemed to be in the act of trying to cock the pistol but seemed not to have strength enough to do it. Fly walked toward Clanton. I went with him. Fly reached down and took hold of the pistol and took it out of Billy's hand. As he did so. Billy Clanton said, 'Give me some more cartridges.' "

Shootouts such as the O.K. Corral gunfight were not as common as western legend has us believe. The men who used their sixguns were not cowboys, but lawmen, outlaws, and men who made their living by gambling or thievery. Tombstone was one of the towns that attracted such men. Its reputation for violence was so well known that the year after the famous gunfight, President Arthur threatened to impose martial law on the entire county.

Fly was presumably acquainted with the Earps, Holliday and such other Tombstone residents as Bat Masterson, Luke Short, Johnny Ringo, and Frank Leslie. He took a group photograph of several of these men when they were on their way to Dodge City as "Peace Commissioners."

Fly focused his camera on other exciting events of Tombstone history. He recorded the destruction wrought by two major fires. One, in 1881, started with the explosion of a barrel of bad whiskey and leveled sixty-six buildings in the town. The following year, a second fire again leveled the heart of the city. In 1883, a gang of men killed four persons in the robbery of the Goldwater and Cateneda dry goods store in nearby Bisbee. The culprits were apprehended and taken to the Tombstone jail. Fly recorded their executions, as well as a few summary vigilante executions over the years.

Through the violent years, the Flys were bastions of the respectable element in the community. A woman who boarded with them recalled, "The Flys were kind, good people. I never heard them say an unkind word about anyone or do an unkind act. They were very kind to one another." But they must have wished at times for a little more money, recalled the boarder: "The Flys lived very plainly, spent almost nothing on themselves and paid cash for everything. Mrs. Fly always kept a little unfinished retouching at hand, and when people had stayed long enough, she referred to her work in an apologetic way."

Fly worked hard, trying to find that main chance. Most summers, his wife tended the gallery in Tombstone collecting fees of 35¢ and up for studio portraits. Fly, meanwhile, was roaming the surrounding countryside, gathering pictures and searching for ore. The local newspaper, the Tombstone *Epitaph*, reported: "One of Tombstone's most persistent miners is Mr. C. S. Fly, the Fremont Street photographer. He has for the last two years put a large share of his earnings . . . into the various prospects around the country. . . . Two years ago he . . . sunk a shaft to a depth of 80 feet with no good results."

Fly's reputation as a photographer increased. In 1885, his pictures were part of the Arizona exhibit at the New Orleans Fair. The following year his pictures of Geronimo's camp brought him national fame and for a time money, from the sale of copies. In 1887, Fly traveled south to take pictures of the great earthquake in Bavispe, Mexico. In 1892, he took a series of pictures of the Chiricahua Mountains, which were later exhibited in London.

But in 1893, hard times shook the country, reaching even to Tombstone. Fly, leaving his wife once more to operate the "home" gallery, set up a new studio in Phoenix, but the venture lasted only about a year. In 1894, he returned to Tombstone, now a more sedate town than it had been the decade before, and was elected sheriff of the county.

Fly's term as sheriff was relatively uneventful, except for the robbery of the Bank of Nogales in 1896. The robbers, bearing such picturesque names as Black Jack Christian and Three-fingered Jack Dunlap, were pursued by posses from two counties, including one led by Sheriff Fly. The outlaws caught the posses in an ambush, and the gang escaped to Mexico. Fly was unhurt, though two other lawmen were injured. But the incident indicated that as a lawman, as one of his friends later wrote, Fly made a "top hand photographer."

Fly retired as sheriff in 1896 and returned to the pursuit of the riches that had always escaped him. He bought a ranch in the Chiricahua Mountains, called Fly's Park, and opened a photographic gallery at Bisbee.

Suffering from depression, Fly died at fifty-one in Bisbee in 1901. His wife brought out a book with his classic pictures of Geronimo in 1903, and continued to operate the Tombstone gallery until it was destroyed by fire in 1912. Many of Fly's plates were destroyed in the fire, and more were lost in warehouses and archives in later years.

CAMILLUS S. FLY: A game of faro at the Orient Saloon at Bisbee, Arizona. Some of the participants and observers are identified as the Dutch Kid, Sleepy Dick, and Tony Downs (third man from left, standing), part owner of the saloon. The dealer is Johnny Murphy, and Smiley Lewis is in the silk hat. National Archives

Today, one of the mountains that he photographed so often in the Chiricahua Mountains is named Fly's Peak in his honor.

The real work of the cowboys of the West was not exercising their trigger fingers. The cowboy was a hardworking ranch hand, skilled at breaking horses for the saddle, roping and branding calves, and keeping track of a herd of wayward cattle. Once or twice a year, in the spring or fall, the cowboy moved his employer's herd on a long and dangerous trip to the nearest railhead. In one of the towns that marked the end of a cattle drive, the cowboy got his pay and was free to find whatever entertainment the town offered. He might even have his picture taken in one of the frontier galleries. Then it was back to work. It was a hard life, and few photographers made a record of range life.

One Texas photographer who made a record of the cattle ranches and the nearby towns was McArthur Cullen Ragsdale. He was born in South Carolina in 1849, and acquired his first camera when he was twenty-one. Ragsdale made a living taking photographs in the Carolinas, and saved his money to attend college. Unfortunately, the bank where he deposited his savings failed, and he left college and headed west.

Ragsdale arrived in the town of Belton, Texas, in 1868. With Belton as a base, he traveled the circuit of Texas towns, northwest to Brownwood and south to Ft. McKavett, Mason, and Fredericksburg. At times, he would be as long as two years gone from his home gallery.

In 1875, Ragsdale settled in a village called St. Angela, near Ft. Concho, where the garrison was still engaged in war with the Plains Indians. Ragsdale made views of Indians, soldiers, and scenes of the St. Angela community. He stayed in St. Angela, married, and continued in the photographic business for forty-seven years, as St. Angela grew into the modern city of San Angelo. In 1915, he sold the business to another photographer, who promptly "cleaned up" the gallery by discarding the thousands of glass plates Ragsdale had made of the frontier over nearly half a century. Legend has it that when Ragsdale learned of the fate of his collection, he ran the new photographer out of town. Ragsdale lived to the ripe old age of ninety-five.

The work of L. A. Huffman on the northern Plains was better preserved, and gives us a comprehensive record of cattle drives and ranch work in the north. After he set up his studio at Miles City in 1878, Huffman spent the next three years photographing the buffalo hide hunters who roamed the area north of the Yellowstone River that Huffman called "the Big Open."

Huffman arrived just in time to photograph the vast herds of buffalo that had once covered the Plains by the millions. According to eyewitnesses, some herds were so large that a rider on horseback could ride for hours to pass by the milling, huge animals. By 1883, white hunters had driven the buffalo close to extinction. The

157

LATON A. HUFFMAN: *Some of the last of the giant buffalo that had been the primary food source for the Plains Indians. A few protected herds remain today in such places as Yellowstone National Park.* Coffrin's Old West Gallery

wholesale slaughter of millions of buffalo for their hides and sometimes only for the sheer thrill of killing was encouraged by the army, which realized that the buffalo was the chief element in the Indians' food supply.

In 1880, Huffman and a partner bought some cattle and started a ranch. Huffman kept up with the latest in photographic techniques, and by the mid-1880s he was using the new "dry-plate" process. Besides disencumbering the photographer of the hundreds of pounds of equipment he formerly carried, the dry-plate process also enabled him to make "instantaneous" views easily. Faster emulsions used on dry plates could stop the action of moving cattle, buffalo, or riders. Huffman even began taking pictures from horseback, something undreamed of in wet-plate days. Nonetheless, it was still a formidable achievement to manipulate a fifty-pound camera from the saddle.

Miles City was an important stop of the Northern Pacific Railroad and became the "Dodge City of the North." Huffman recorded the cattle drives, the cowboys, and the life of an end-of-the-trail town. A rancher now himself, he was in a unique position to photograph life on the open range. He photographed many scenes of cowboys at work, and often left explanatory captions.

Huffman also was a careful craftsman, telling of one picture that took him more than a week of "riding, watching, and waiting." Fortunately, almost his entire collection of plates has been preserved in a gallery in Miles City.

For fifty-two years, Huffman operated galleries in Montana. He occasionally was elected to public office, such as county commissioner or member of the state legislature. For a brief period

LATON A. HUFFMAN: This is one of a series of photos Huffman made showing the steps in breaking a horse to the saddle. Coffrin's Old West Gallery

between 1890 and 1896 he tried his luck in Chicago, but the frontier called him back, and he returned to Billings, and finally Miles City. He photographed one of the very last of the open range cattle drives in 1904. He continued to sell prints and stereos of his photographs until his death in 1931.

Overshadowed by his photographs of ranching and buffalo hunting are Huffman's views of Miles City, as it grew from mining camp to small twentieth-century city. Many other photographers

160

J. C. H. GRABILL: Grabill's description of this scene was: "Villa of Brule. The great hostile Indian camp on River Brule near Pine Ridge, S.D." Since the date of the picture is thought to be 1891, the description "hostile" was probably intended to stimulate sales of stereo cards in the East. National Archives

made similar records of the communities in which they worked. Unfortunately, in many cases, all that remains is the photographer's name and some of his plates.

J. C. H. Grabill took memorable views of the tough mining town of Deadwood, Dakota Territory, where Wild Bill Hickock met his end. Grabill's scenes include Indian and army life, ranching, mining, and the stage routes that came through the Dakota Territory.

E. E. Henry, based in Leavenworth, Kansas, made an important collection of frontier views in the sixties and seventies, during the time when the Kansas Pacific Railroad was being built. He photographed many of the soldiers from nearby Ft. Riley, including George A. Custer, when he was active on the southern Plains.

The careers of the photographers of Colorado are better known. The discovery of gold in the Pikes Peak region in 1858 brought many miners into the area and resulted in mushrooming boom towns where photographers set up business.

George D. Wakely was working in Denver in 1859, when it was still called "Russell's Settlement," after the first discoverer of gold. Wakely and his wife had arrived in the city as part of a traveling

GEORGE D. WAKELY: Traveling troupes of actors and entertainers usually brought the whole town and surrounding farmers and ranchers in to see the show. Mlle. Carolista is seen here performing her tightrope act over Larimer Street. **Denver Public Library Western History Department**

theater troupe. His pictures show a flair for the theatrical, and one taken in 1861 shows a female tightrope walker, Mlle. Carolista, walking a wire suspended over Larimer Street. Wakely sold his Denver gallery in 1864. Fifteen years later, he turned up in the boom camp of Leadville, again as a photographer. Some of his best pictures are of the mountain scenery of Colorado.

Central City, a rival to Denver in its early years, boasted a "daguerrean and sign painting" business owned by Henry Faul and Mark Allyn in 1861. Faul dropped Allyn and continued to operate a succession of galleries in the ensuing years. He is notable for taking the first photograph in Colorado of a public hanging. Newspaper records show that the prisoner had attempted to commit suicide in his cell by breaking the glass covering of a daguerreotype of his family and slashing his wrists.

William G. Chamberlain was a prolific photographer who opened business in Denver in 1861. He was then forty-six years old, and had learned daguerreotyping when he left his Massachusetts home to see the world. In Lima, Peru, he met two Americans making a photographic tour of Chile and Peru. They sold him their equipment and taught him how to use it for $300. He set up a photographic business in Chicago in 1855, and came west seeking gold four years later.

Chamberlain set up a branch studio in Central City in 1864, under the supervision of Frank Danielson. The evidence indicates that Chamberlain was one of the more successful early photographers. His motto of "A good picture or no pay" brought him many customers and good notices in the local newspapers, one of which editorialized that doctors in the area should adopt a parallel motto.

Chamberlain's wife was also a capable photographer, and filled in for her husband while he made an annual tour of the mountain regions to acquire stereo views. On the opening of Chamberlain's enlarged Denver gallery in 1872, the local newspaper described it in appreciative detail. "Mr. Chamberlain," the account said, "operates seven cameras, one of which, wrought in exquisite form and valued at $125, and named the 'multiplying box,' has the marvelous capacity of taking . . . seventy-two pictures at one sitting."

The "multiplying box" was used for taking *cartes de visite*, small pictures about 3½" × 2". *Cartes de visite* were used as calling cards and mounted in family albums, and were often ordered in quantities—hence the need for a camera that could take seventy-two of them at once. The entire plate of seventy-two pictures would be printed on a single sheet of photographic paper. The prints were then cut apart and pasted on individual cards.

Chamberlain's large series of stereo views of Colorado scenery, Indians, pioneers, and town life sold for the relatively high price of $12 to $15 a dozen. He could command the price because his series was exceptional for the variety and quality of the views. Chamberlain's gallery burned in 1874, but not all the views were lost, for he continued to sell stereos until 1881, when his eyesight failed him.

W. Delavan, a deaf-mute artist, arrived in Colorado in 1868. He was engaged in making one of the popular "panoramas," similar to the one J. Wesley Jones had completed earlier. Delavan, making photographs along the Union Pacific line as models for his paintings, planned a canvas with a hundred scenes from Omaha to San Francisco. Each scene on the canvas would be 6' × 10'. The Union Pacific Co. had subscribed enough money to the project to ensure that Denver would be represented by at least six scenes, but a local Denver newspaper, fearing that towns such as "Cheyenne, Laramie, Central, Georgetown, or Golden City" might have greater space on the canvas, appealed to the civic pride of local businessmen to subscribe even more.

While Delavan was in Denver, a mob lynched a suspected criminal, and the local newspaper feared the effect such lawlessness might have on Denver's reputation. Referring to the body hanging from a cottonwood tree, the editor wrote: "We are told that certain artists were nigh fighting over it this morning for the exclusive privilege of taking photographic views of it. Denver, after eight years of freedom from lynch law, seems destined to figure in Mr. Delavan's Panorama of the World as the rival in lawlessness of the worst of the railroad towns."

The Rocky Mountains provided a rich lode for photographers seeking scenic gold. The firm of Williams and McDonald of Denver took the first photographs of the area around the present-day Rocky Mountain National Park in the late 1860s. The Duhem brothers of Denver operated a gallery from 1869 to 1877, and advertised a collection of 300 stereo views of what was called "the wild scenery of the 'Switzerland of America.'"

Joseph Collier, a Scot, arrived in Central City in 1871, when he was thirty-five years old. He had been trained as a blacksmith, but an injury sent him into the photographic trade. He stayed in Central City until 1878, when he opened a studio in Denver, which he operated until two years before his death in 1910. He took views of the interior of the Caribou mine, mule trains, and ranching activities, in addition to his gallery and town photographs.

Numerous stereo cards of Colorado and surrounding states were offered for sale by Charles Weitfle, who emigrated from Germany at the age of thirteen in 1849. In 1856, he made a photographic tour of Brazil, and was operating a gallery in Washington, D.C., when the Civil War broke out. He served as a photographer with the Union Army and after the war ran a gallery in New Jersey. He came to Colorado in 1878, lured by the gold strikes.

Weitfle bought up the work of such photographers as the Duhem brothers and Chamberlain, among others, and incorporated them in his stereo series. He himself was a prolific photographer, and made a series of views of Utah communities, and the mining camps and attractions of Colorado. In the early 1880s he moved his studio to Denver, where he published stereo cards by the thousands. A gallery fire destroyed his life's work—along with the glass plates of other photographers—in 1883. What became of him after that is unknown.

The most famous photographer who worked in Denver was W. H. Jackson, who, in his ninety-nine-year life span, covered all the important areas of the West and much of the rest of the world as well. After the end of the Hayden surveys, in 1878, Jackson set himself up in business on Larimer Street in Denver.

In 1881, the Denver and Rio Grande Railway Company commissioned Jackson to photograph the line, which was ambitiously projected as running from Denver to Mexico City. The railroad ran special trains, called "Jackson Specials" for the use of their photographer, equipped with a flat car to serve as a platform for his cameras. As the growing web of railroads spread through the West, Jackson took his cameras into new territory. His eye never became jaded from so much scenery, and many classic Jackson views were taken during this period.

In 1892, Jackson and a partner photographed the Columbian

Exposition in Chicago, with its miles of exhibits. An album of a hundred 11" × 14" Jackson pictures of the Exposition sold at the time for $1,000. This was a small fortune, but Jackson was quite possibly the most famous photographer in the United States by this time.

After the exposition the World's Transportation Commission and Field Columbian Museum paid Jackson to undertake a seventeen-month tour of the world, making photographs of historic interest. Jackson trained his lens on Europe, North Africa, India, China, Japan, and Siberia.

Despite his world-renowned reputation, Jackson found himself in financial difficulty as a result of the Panic of 1893, and he sold his company to the Detroit Publishing Co., where he became a director. In his later years, he continued his photographic work, making pictures and prints for Photochrom Co., a manufacturer of post-cards. In the last quarter-century of his long life, Jackson returned to his earlier avocation of painting. He made murals and canvases of the western scenes he had recorded on glass plates years before.

Remembering his early years as a gallery photographer in Omaha, Jackson summed up the kind of work a local photographer was most often called on to do: "straight portrait jobs; group pictures of lodges, church societies and political clubs; and outdoor shots that gratified civic pride. There were many commissions to photograph shop fronts, and occasionally, interiors. Now and then, too, somebody would order pictures of his new house; or of his big barn, and along with it the livestock."

Jackson's wanderlust made him dissatisfied with that kind of work, but other photographers spent their entire lives doing it. Some few were able to live long enough to build collections of local views that were as important as the more spectacular photos that men like Jackson did.

One of the most brilliant careers of a local photographer was that of Peter Britt, who in fifty years of business in Jacksonville, Oregon, seldom strayed more than 200 miles from his gallery. Yet not only did Britt build a fascinating record of the growth of a western town, but he was himself partly responsible for Jacksonville's survival as a community.

The year after his arrival, Britt helped to establish a supply trail to the port of Crescent City, California. For several years, he earned a

PETER BRITT: The first photograph of Crater Lake, made in 1874. Southern Oregon Historical Society

living outfitting pack trains. In 1859, he left that business, and began building a house in which he would live and operate his photographic studio until after the turn of the century. He brought a young widow from Illinois to become his wife, adopted her young son, and fathered a boy and a girl. As the children grew older, Britt would pack them in a wagon with cameras and supplies and wander through the region photographing the changes and growth and natural wonders of the northwest country.

Britt was the first to photograph Oregon's 1,900-foot-deep Crater Lake, in 1874. His son Emil recalled that several men accompanied the photographic party, "All westerners are used to camp life except one, a rather prominent man who was visiting in Jacksonville and wanted to go along." The prominent man had a harder journey than he expected. The wagon could only be used for part of the trip, and mules had to be used to carry the supplies up to the rim of the crater surrounding the lake. When the party arrived, the weather was too cloudy for Britt to make a picture. Britt and his companions endured a cold steady rain that went on for three days. With provisions running low and the party thoroughly wet and cold, Britt decided that they would begin the return trip the next morning. Fortunately, the rain stopped just in time for Britt to make a series of magnificent views of the lake. Conservationists used the Britt pictures to persuade Congress to establish Crater Lake National Park in 1902.

Jacksonville had a sizable Chinese population, which Britt photographed and treated with as much respect as his other neighbors. He gave financial support to Chinese looking to reopen abandoned gold claims, and allowed a Chinese company to mine on his own property.

The restrictive lending policies of the bank of Jacksonville eventually led Britt to use his own money to finance many settlers who wanted to homestead or set up business in the community. His generosity brought him wealth in the form of land put up for collateral. By the time of his death, he owned more land in southern Oregon than any other single individual.

Most importantly for the community, Britt attempted to prove that almost any crop could grow in what he considered to be the temperate climate of Jacksonville. He imported many plants, including grapevines, peach, apple, and pear trees to the area and grew them successfully. His homemade wines were sold to neighbors and to visitors to the gallery who came through on the stage line. The news that fruits and vines could grow in the region attracted publicity.

The family photographic business was continued by Britt's son Emil when the old man retired at the age of eighty-one. But Peter Britt continued to work on behalf of his beloved community. He died in 1905 after a strenuous trip to Portland, where he presided over an exhibit of the products and resources of southern Oregon—fruit, wine, minerals, and photographs that Britt had taken. The most remarkable resource, though, was Peter Britt himself.

* * *

Salt Lake City was fortunate in having several prolific photographers to record its early history. Besides its first daguerreotypist, Marsena Cannon, there were Charles R. Savage, who first worked in Cannon's gallery, and Charles William Carter.

Carter had served as a soldier in the British army during the Crimean War. Afterward, he worked as a school teacher in Britain, with photography as a sideline. He became a convert to Mormonism, and came to Utah in 1859. He purchased photographic equipment, probably from Cannon, and set himself up in business. Around 1863, he opened "Carter's View Emporium," on East Temple Street, then the newest and most fashionable commercial section of town.

The Mormon leader, Brigham Young, was interested in photography. The Mormons' beliefs include a special historical consciousness, since they believe it is possible to obtain salvation for one's ancestors, and careful historical records and research are kept in the church archives. Thus it was a special triumph for Cannon when Brigham Young came to his studio to have his portrait taken.

Carter also went beyond the walls of his studio to capture many views of the growing community. He took a series of views of the Salt Lake Temple and Tabernacle, from its early stages to the dedication. He photographed Indians in the area, and federal troops at nearby Camp Douglas. His active career continued through the turn of the century, when he sold his collection of some 2,000 negatives to the Bureau of Information of the Mormon Church, where it lay preserved yet forgotten until a curator discovered part of it in 1963. Carter died at age eighty-five in 1918.

Savage operated his Pioneer Art Gallery on East Temple Street from the time he took it over from Marsena Cannon in 1861 until his retirement in 1906. The year after Savage became famous for his presence at the driving of the last spike of the railroad, he received the semi-official approval of Brigham Young. Young chose Savage to accompany him on a trip to photograph the Mormon settlements in southern Utah.

Savage was a successful businessman, and active in the life of his church and community. He also traveled through the Utah area with his one-time partner, the artist George M. Ottinger, making photographs and sketches. Savage's series of stereo views along the railroad and of Utah scenery was popular throughout the country.

CHARLES W. CARTER: A Mormon wagon train around 1879. National Archives

The Mormon Church came under attack from the government of the United States for certain of its tenets, including the provision allowing polygamy. In the "wooden gun rebellion" of 1870, Savage and his assistant James Fennemore were arrested and charged with treason when they were part of a military band that paraded in a town square with wooden guns. Savage wrote a song about the affair while under arrest at Ft. Douglas.

Later, Savage, who had four wives, was in danger of prosecution

CHARLES R. SAVAGE: The pair of pictures shown here made up one entire stereo card. Viewed with a stereoscope, the image appeared in three dimensions. Skilled photographers like Savage sought to enhance the three-dimensional view by composing their pictures with an eye for depth, as in this picture. The photographer's darkroom wagon is seen in the background. The Metropolitan Museum of Art, Gift of Weston Naef, 1975

under the Anti-polygamy Edmunds Bill of 1883. His American citizenship was taken from him, but he remained out of prison, unlike some of his fellow church members. He photographed them in prison, where he went to preach the Mormon gospel.

During the seventies and eighties, while judicial persecution of the Church continued, Savage photographed for the Union Pacific and Denver and Rio Grande western railroads. He issued his series of stereo "Views of the Great West" from the results of these trips. The railroads used his pictures in postcards and travel folders. The high repute that Savage held nationally as a photographer can be inferred from the fact that the railroads obviously valued his services, despite the anti-Mormon feeling that had spread through Congress and the rest of the nation.

A fire in the summer of 1883 wiped out Savage's collection of early wet-plate views. He responded by taking up the new dry-plate technology and beginning a new series of pictures of Salt Lake City and vicinity.

By Christmas of 1883, Savage had reopened his business, now called the Art Bazaar, and advertised a collection of congratulatory telegrams that had reportedly been sent by such notables as President Chester Arthur, Kaiser Wilhelm of Germany, Queen Victoria, and the King of the Sandwich Islands (Hawaii). The wry humor that indicates the "telegrams" were in fact written by Savage can be seen in the text of President Arthur's message: "Sorry I cannot get time to go to Utah this year, but will be sure to give you a call when I do come." This was during a decade when Congress was actively seeking to destroy the Church of which Savage was still a devout member.

A new Church president, Wilford Woodruff, finally made peace with Congress in 1890, urging all members to comply with the laws of the United States regarding marriage. Two years later, Savage photographed the gala occasion of the completion of the Mormon Temple in Salt Lake City. It had been thirty-nine years since Marsena Cannon had photographed the laying of the cornerstone.

The following year, Savage entered a display of his landscapes in the Columbian Exposition and World's Fair in Chicago. He also attended the fair as a member of the Mormon Tabernacle Choir, which won a prize for its performance.

When Savage retired from his gallery in 1906, he left an extensive record of the growth of a frontier community and church that had to battle religious persecution and near-warfare to survive.

Some photographers recorded not only a single city, but roamed over a wide territory. Stanley J. Morrow's photographs show the lives and work of the pioneers along the Missouri River frontier. In his darkroom wagon he photographed scenes along the river from Sioux City, Iowa, to Helena, Montana. Yankton—Morrow's home—was an important stop for the river traffic and Morrow's pictures include many views of steamboats and river workers.

As he traveled, Morrow's practice was to set up his wagon in the towns and military camps en route. There usually was no resident

STANLEY J. MORROW: *A miner guards his claim at a prospecting site near Deadwood, around 1876, when the discovery of gold brought thousands of prospectors into the area.* W. H. Over Museum, University of South Dakota

photographer in these places, and Morrow was able to capture enough business to make his trips profitable. His photographic views of places where no other photographer had been, sold in the form of stereo cards, brought him additional work. He began to get commissions from eastern publications that wanted photographs for their engravers to use as models for illustrations. The New York *Daily Graphic* and *Frank Leslie's Illustrated Newspaper* paid him for pictures of miners and wagon trains traveling to the Black Hills. His shot of the Gray-Gordon expedition, in 1876, was extensively reproduced.

Morrow took many views of the mining towns of the Dakotas. His views, sometimes repeated at a later date, show the rapid growth and sometimes the decline of the towns, as well as the effect mining operations had on the surrounding wilderness. A local newspaper recorded the swift progress: "Six weeks ago the site of Deadwood was a heavy forest of pine timber, now it extends nearly a mile along Deadwood and Whitewood, and contains nearly two thousand of the most energetic driving people on the continent." As the miners flowed into the area, Morrow's camera recorded the hills stripped of trees and piles of slag rising throughout the valleys.

After Morrow opened branch galleries at Ft. Keogh and Ft. Custer, his wife and several assistants operated the Yankton gallery during his absences. Their work was taking the portraits and typical town views that were the mainstay of a photographer's living. In 1881, the Morrow gallery photographed the huge ice breakup in the Missouri River that crushed steamboats and caused a flood in Yankton. The flood was so severe that some of the riverboats were left stranded nearly half a mile from the riverbank when it subsided.

Morrow's wife was in poor health by the early 1880s, and the family traveled to Florida. Sale of the Morrow stereo views, titled "Photographic Gems of the Great Northwest" were sufficient to permit the Morrows a comfortable life. Morrow traveled through the South, continuing his photography until his death in Dallas in 1921.

Another substantial record of a large portion of the frontier was made by Frank Jay Haynes, in his unique position as official photographer of the Union Pacific Railroad. For more than twenty-one years the Haynes Palace Car traveled along the rails. Haynes was the first and sometimes the only photographer to make a record of many of the early communities of the Northwest. The economic security he got from his position gave him the freedom to go farther afield and photograph places that brought no immediate profit—in many cases, the towns that had gone bust after the boom and no longer contained any paying customers.

In 1876 Haynes, then a young man of twenty-three, set up his first studio in Moorhead, Minnesota. Not long after, he married Lily V. Snyder. She must have realized her husband had the wanderlust when he traveled to Bismarck and Deadwood soon after to take photographs.

By the end of 1879, "Professor" Haynes—as he was already calling himself—had moved his wife and business to Fargo. He brought more to the citizens of Fargo than photographic skill. In his gallery, he also sold "Rogers statuettes" of "classic" figures such as Romeo and Juliet, Mozart, and President Grant. His other wares included sheet music, organs, and a variety of other musical instruments.

Haynes also traveled along the Missouri River and its tributaries, photographing not only the faces of the people, but every conceivable activity that might be of interest. He never seemed to miss an opportunity for a photograph, whether he was waiting at an isolated station for the next stage to arrive, or spending an extra hour at one of the countless frontier settlements that sprang up along the railroads and river. Indians, soldiers, miners, scouts, tradespeople, traders, riverboat workers . . . all these and more were subjects for Haynes's camera. He photographed the Northwest from St. Paul to Idaho, and to our great good luck, virtually all of his photographs were cataloged and preserved.

If there was such a thing as a "society" photographer in the Northwest, Haynes filled that role, too. In 1883 he went with President Chester A. Arthur's party to Yellowstone. It was not just a little camping trip—Arthur "roughed it" with one hundred seventy-five pack animals to carry provisions and camping gear. But there was a total press blackout on the affair. No reporters, and no photographers except Haynes were permitted—an arrangement that gave Professor Haynes a triumphant "scoop." His pictures were much in demand by every illustrated publication in the country.

In 1880, Haynes secured the concessionary right to make and sell photographs of Yellowstone National Park. He prepared for this venture by equipping himself with the new dry-plate technology. He used numerous cameras in his work of photographing the park. One was a stereo camera that had three sets of interchangeable lenses, for close-up to long-focus views. Biggest of the cameras was a 20″ × 24″ Scovill model, with a lens made by the German firm of Voigtlander and Sons. On one occasion, Haynes had the ninety-two-pound monster lowered on ropes to the bottom of the Lower Falls of the Yellowstone to make a photograph there.

Over the years, Haynes took thousands of photographs of the park. His stereo views were bought and brought back home by

FRANK J. HAYNES: *The Indian welcoming party for President Arthur at Yellowstone National Park in 1883. The umbrellas were badges of rank accorded to chiefs.* The Haynes Foundation

virtually every family that visited the park in the early years. The images he took helped to enshrine the park in the pantheon of familiar images of America. It became one of the places that every American was aware of—like Niagara Falls and the Statue of Liberty. Haynes turned the business over to his son in 1916, but the original F. J. Haynes views continued to sell as stereos or postcards for years afterward.

Attracted by Haynes's pictures, a growing number of tourists began to visit the park, and Haynes capitalized on the tourism in his other business ventures. He was a partner in two stage lines that

brought tourists from the railroad to the park. When E. H. Harriman, the railroad magnate, came to visit, Haynes guided him through the park with his customary enthusiasm. At the end, the taciturn Harriman reportedly said, "Mr. Haynes, I must have some of this tourist business." Soon after, the Union Pacific built a branch line from Pocatello, Idaho, to the Yellowstone.

Haynes died in 1920, and in tribute to his accomplishments, a peak on the western entrance route to the park was named Mt. Haynes.

* * *

The end of the frontier, if it had a date, came at noon, April 22, 1889, when Congress—violating yet another Indian treaty—permitted white settlers to stake claims in the Indian Territory, today's Oklahoma. Within a few hours claim signs went up on over two million acres of land, and the population of a place that would be called Oklahoma City went from zero to 10,000. There to record the events and the final settlement of the frontier was H. T. Swearingen.

Others sensed that the end of the frontier was at hand and set out consciously to record as much of it as they could. Solomon D. Butcher, who had been born in West Virginia in 1856, spent twenty years making a photographic history of life on the Great Plains. Butcher learned the photographer's trade as a young man and spent some time as a traveling photographer in Illinois. He came west with his parents in March, 1880, and filed a claim in Custer County, Nebraska. Later giving up the claim, he went to Minneapolis for medical college, but found "I had seen enough of the Wild West to unfit me for ever living contentedly in the East." With his new bride, he returned to Custer County, where he set up a photographic gallery. He later moved to Walworth, which seemed to offer a greater opportunity.

It was in 1886, when he was thirty, that Butcher conceived his idea of making a pioneer history. He would record the experiences of the settlers in a book illustrated with photographs of them and their homes. For seven years, Butcher traveled around the county photographing and collecting personal histories. Then a fire wiped out most of his printed materials. He saved the glass plates, and began again. Eventually, he collected over 1,500 pictures.

Butcher photographed his pioneer families as they chose. Most of them preferred to stand or sit, face-on to the camera, with their houses, children, pets, and possessions around them. They had conquered the land, and were proud of it.

Butcher could find no publisher for his vast labor of love, and a local rancher raised a subscription to pay for the book's publication in an edition of a thousand copies. Butcher's photographs reside today in the Nebraska State Historical Society, a priceless heritage.

Evelyn Jephson Cameron first saw Montana on her honeymoon in 1889. She and her husband, Ewen, came back later to settle. He was

SOLOMON D. BUTCHER: The Moses Speese Family in front of their sod house, windmill, wagons, and horses. Ex-slaves were among the pioneers who came West seeking a better life. Solomon D. Butcher Collection, Nebraska State Historical Society

a naturalist, and she was the photographer. She made a collection of frontier life, developing and printing her pictures in the darkroom in their house, which the Camerons shared with two pet wolves. The technical innovations of dry-plate photography enabled her to photograph interiors of cabins and houses, illustrating the domestic details which are missing from early photographers' work.

Erwin E. Smith was a Texas wrangler who learned to manipulate his dry-plate camera on horseback. His action photographs of the cattle drives and ranch work are among the most exciting ever taken in the West, though all of his work was done after 1900.

179

F. A. Rinehart was the owner of a successful portrait studio in Omaha when the Trans-Mississippi and International Exposition took place there in 1898. Appointed official photographer for the Exposition, Rinehart photographed many of the Indians who came to the Fair for an Indian Congress. He became absorbed in this work and continued collecting photographs of the Indians, mostly studio views, showing the native Americans in ceremonial dress. Eventually, his collection numbered over 1,200 pictures that show, as one critic has written, "a captured people, taken at a moment in history when they had ceased to be a threat and were beginning their long career as a subject of myth, romance, and guilt in the American imagination."

The most extensive collection of Indians on the reservation was made by Edward S. Curtis, who set out to make a comprehensive record of the culture and characteristics of the Indians of North America. From 1900 to 1930, he visited more than 80 tribes, taking more than 40,000 pictures of Indians. His collection is magnificent, for Curtis had a dramatic flair for pose and lighting, but the Indians he portrayed already had begun to fill the role of myth. Curtis's photographs show the spirit of the Indians as it was romanticized by their conquerers. The pictures are exceptional works of art, but they could not portray the real Indian, or the real West. The real West was gone, but not before its photographers had captured a part of it on silver and glass for us to see.

F. A. RINEHART: A man and woman from the Apache tribes posing before a painted backdrop in Rinehart's studio. The costumes and the cartridge belt were only ceremonial remembrances of the Indian way of life and the frontier, now gone for good. Prakapas Gallery

BONY TELA   HATTIE TOM
SAN CARLOS — APACHES — CHIRICAHUA

BIBLIOGRAPHY

Information on the photographers of the frontier is scattered throughout historical journals and archives. New information about them turns up every year as people increasingly realize the importance of those men and women who made a record of the American frontier. The starting place for anyone seeking to find information about America's nineteenth-century photographers will probably always be Professor Robert Taft's *Photography and the American Scene.*

Andrews, Ralph W., *Indians as the Westerners Saw Them*, Bonanza Books, New York, 1963.

————, *Photographers of the Frontier West*, Bonanza Books, New York, 1965.

————, *Picture Gallery Pioneers*, 1850–1875, Bonanza Books, New York, 1964.

Bartlett, Richard A., *Great Surveys of the American West*, University of Oklahoma Press, Norman, 1962.

Bell, William A., *New Tracks in North America*, 1965 edition, Horn & Wallace Publishers, Albuquerque, N.M.; 1870 edition, Scribner, Walford & Co., New York.

Bell, William, "Photography in the Grand Gulch of the Colorado River," *The Philadelphia Photographer*, Vol. X, 1873.

Belous, Russell E. and Weinstein, Robert A., *Will Soule: Indian Photographer at Fort Sill, Oklahoma 1869–74*, The Ward Ritchie Press, Los Angeles, 1973.

Bendix, Howard E., "Discovered!! Early Bierstadt Photographs," *Photographica*, Vol. VII, 1975.

Brown, Dee, *Bury My Heart at Wounded Knee*, Holt, Rinehart, and Winston, New York, 1970.

————, *Hear That Lonesome Whistle Blow*, Bantam Books, New York, 1978.

Brown, Mark H., and Felton, W. R., *Before Barbed Wire: L. A. Huffman, Photographer on Horseback*, Henry Holt & Co., New York, 1956.

————, *The Frontier Years: L. A. Huffman, Photographer of the Plains*, Bramhall House, New York, 1955.

Burdick, Usher L., ed., "David F. Barry's Indian Notes on the Custer Battle," Wirth Brothers, Baltimore, 1949.

Butcher, Solomon D., *Pioneer History of Custer County, Nebraska*, introduction by Harry E. Chrisman, Sage Books, Denver, 1965

Carvalho, Solomon Nunes, *Incidents of Travel and Adventure in the Far West*, ed. with introduction by Bertram Wallace Korn, The Jewish Publication Society of America, Philadelphia, 1954.

Cobb, Josephine, "Alexander Gardner," *Image*, Vol. VII, No. 6, June, 1958.

Combs, Barry B., *Westward to Promontory*, Promontory Press, New York, 1969.

Darrah, William Culp, "Beaman, Fennemore, Hillers, Dellenbaugh, Johnson and Hattan," *Utah Historical Quarterly*, Vol. XVI–XVII (1948–49).

———, *The World of Stereographs*, W. C. Darrah, pub., Gettysburg, Pa., 1978.

Fardon, G. R., *San Francisco in the 1850's, views by G. R. Fardon*, introduction by Robert A. Sobieszek, Dover Publications, Inc., New York, 1977.

Fly, Mrs. M. E., *Scenes in Geronimo's Camp; the Apache Outlaw and Murderer*, Tombstone, Ariz., n.d. (190?).

Frink, Maurice, with Casey E. Barthelmess, *Photographer on an Army Mule*, University of Oklahoma Press, Norman, 1965.

Frost, Lawrence A., "General Custer's Photographers," *The (Chicago) Westerner's Brand Book*, V. XXI, No. 8, Oct., 1964.

Gardner's Photographic Sketchbook of the Civil War, Dover Publications, Inc., New York, Introduction by E. F. Bleiler, 1959.

Glover, Ridgway, "Photography Among the Indians," *The Philadelphia Photographer*, Vol. III, Aug., Oct., Dec., 1866.

Goetzmann, William H., *Army Exploration in the American West, 1803–1863*, Yale University Press, New Haven, 1959.

———, *Exploration and Empire*, Knopf, New York, 1966.

Goodman, Theodosia Teel, "Early Oregon Daguerreotypers and Portrait Photographers," *Oregon Historical Quarterly*, Vol. XLIX, No. 1, Mar., 1948.

Gray, John S., "Itinerant Frontier Photographers and Images Lost, Strayed, or Stolen," *Montana*, Vol. XXVIII, No. 2, April, 1978.

———, "Photographic Strays and Mavericks," *The (Chicago) Westerner's Brand Book*, June, 1965.

Grenbeaux, Pauline, "Before Yosemite Art Gallery: Watkins' Early Career," *California History*, Vol. LVII, No. 3, Fall, 1978.

Grosscup, Jeffrey P., "William Illingworth: Stereoscopic Eye on the Frontier West," *Montana*, Vol. XXV, No. 2, Spring, 1975.

Haas, Robert Bartlett, *Muybridge: Man in Motion*, Univ. of California Press, Berkeley, 1976.

———, "William Herman Rulofson," *California Historical Society Quarterly*, Vol. XXXIV, No. 4, Dec., 1955; Vol. XXXV, No. 1, Mar., 1956.

Haley, J. Evetts, *Focus on the Frontier*, Shamrock Oil and Gas Corp., Amarillo, Texas, 1957.

Harber, Opal M., "A Few Early Photographers of Colorado," *The Colorado Magazine*, Vol. XXXIII, Oct., 1956.

Hoobler, Dorothy and Thomas, *Photographing History: The Career of Mathew Brady*, G. P. Putnam's Sons, New York, 1977.

Hood, Mary L., "C. L. Weed, Yosemite's First Photographer," *Yosemite Nature Notes*, Vol. XXXVIII, No. 6, June, 1959.

Horan, James D., *Timothy O'Sullivan: America's Forgotten Photographer*, Bonanza Books, New York, 1966.

Hunt, Freda, "The Punishment of Pi-zi's People," *Overland Monthly*, Vol. LV, No. 3, Mar., 1910.

Hurt, Wesley R., and Lass, William E., *Frontier Photographer: Stanley J. Morrow's Dakota Years*, Univ. of South Dakota and Univ. of Nebraska Press, 1956.

"Image of America. Early Photography, 1839–1900." Catalog of Library of Congress exhibition, February 8, 1957, Nelson R. Burr, researcher.

Jackson, Clarence S., *Picture Maker of the Old West*, Charles Scribner's Sons, New York, 1947.

Jackson, William H., *Time Exposure*, Cooper Square Publishers, New York, 1970.

Jackson, William H., and Driggs, Howard R., *The Pioneer Photographer*, World Book Co., Yonkers-on-Hudson, N.Y., 1929.

Jensen, Oliver; Kerr, Joan Paterson; and Belsky, Murray, *American Album*, Ballantine Books, New York, 1968.

Lamar, Howard, ed., *The Reader's Encyclopedia of the American West*, Thomas Y. Crowell Co., New York, 1977.

Lockley, Fred, *Oregon Trail Blazers*, Knickerbocker Press, 1919.

MacDonnell, Kevin, *Eadweard Muybridge, The Man Who Invented the Moving Picture*, Little, Brown & Co., Boston, 1970.

Mayer, Lynne; Mayer, Rhodes; and Vose, Kenneth E., *Makin' Tracks*, Praeger, New York, 1975.

Miller, Alan Clark, "Lorenzo Lorain, Pioneer Photographer of the Northwest," *The American West*, Vol. IX, No. 1, Jan., 1972.

———, *Photographer of a Frontier: The Photographs of Peter Britt*, Interface California Corp., Eureka, Cal., 1976.

Mumie, Dr. Nolie, "William Henry Jackson: A Tribute," *(Denver) Westerner's Brand Book*, Vol. III, 1949.

Naef, Weston J., and Wood, James N., with essay by Heyman, Therese Thau, *Era of Exploration: The Rise of Landscape Photography in the American West, 1860–1885*, New York Graphic Society, Boston, 1975.

Newhall, Beaumont, "Ambulatory Galleries," *Image*, Vol. V, No. 9, Nov., 1956.

————, *The History of Photography from 1839 to the Present Day*, Museum of Modern Art, New York, 1949.

————, "Minnesota Daguerreotypes," *Minnesota History*, Vol. XXXIV, No. 1, Spring, 1954.

Newhall, Beaumont, and Edkins, Diana, *William H. Jackson*, Morgan & Morgan, Dobbs Ferry, N.Y., 1974.

Pattison, William D., "Collector's Choice: The Photographs of A. J. Russell," *The American West*, Vol. VI, No. 3, May, 1969.

————, "The Pacific Railroad Rediscovered," *The Geographical Review*, Vol. LII, No. 1, 1962.

————, "Westward by Rail With Professor Sedgwick: A Lantern Journey of 1873," *Historical Society of Southern California Quarterly*, Vol. XXIV, No. 4, Dec., 1960.

Ravenswaay, Charles van, "The Pioneer Photographers of St. Louis," *Missouri Historical Bulletin*, Vol. X, Oct., 1953.

Reiter, Joan Swallow, *The Women*, Time-Life Books, Alexandria, Va., 1978.

Richmond, Robert W., "Kansas Through a Camera," *The American West*, Vol. II, No. 3.

Rinehart, Floyd, and Rinehart, Marion, *American Daguerreian Art*, Clarkson N. Potter, Inc., New York, 1967.

Rudisill, Richard, *Mirror Image: The Influence of the Daguerreotype on American Society*, Albuquerque, University of New Mexico Press, 1971.

Samson, John, "Photographs from the High Rockies," *Harper's New Monthly Magazine*, No. 232, Sept., 1869.

Savage, Charles R., "A Photographic Tour of Nearly 9000 Miles," *The Philadelphia Photographer*, Vol. IV, Sept., Oct., 1867.

Schmitt, Martin F., and Brown, Dee, *Fighting Indians of the West*, Charles Scribner's Sons, New York, 1948.

————, *The Settlers' West*, Ballantine Books, New York, 1955.

Serven, James E., "C. S. Fly—Tombstone, A.T.," *Arizona Highways*, Vol. XLIV, No. 2, Feb., 1970.

Smith, Erwin E., and Haley, J. Evetts, *Life on the Texas Range*, University of Texas Press, Austin, 1952.

Steward, Julian H., "Notes on Hillers' Photographs of the Paiute and Ute Indians Taken on the Powell Expedition of 1873," *Smithsonian Miscellaneous Collections*, Vol. 98, No. 18, July 21, 1939.

Taft, Robert, "Additional Notes on the Gardner Photographs of Kansas," *Kansas Historical Quarterly*, Vol. VI, No. 2, May, 1937.

————, *Artists and Illustrators of the Old West 1850–1900*, Charles Scribner's Sons, New York, 1953.

————, "John Plumbe, America's First Nationally Known Photographer," *American Photography*, Vol. 30, No. 1, Jan., 1936.

————, *Photography and the American Scene*, Dover Publications, New York, 1964.

Tilden, Freeman, *Following the Frontier with F. J. Haynes*, Knopf, New York, 1964.

"The Tombstone of Camillus S. Fly," *Friends,* Ceco Publishing Co., Detroit, Jan, 1969.

Traywick, Ben T., *Tombstone's Immortals*, 1973.

Turrill, Charles B., "An Early California Photographer: C. E. Watkins," *News Notes of California Libraries*, Vol. XIII, No. 1, Jan., 1918.

Wadsworth, Nelson B., *Through Camera Eyes*, Brigham Univ. Press, Provo, Utah, 1975.

———, "Zion's Cameramen: Early Photographers of Utah and the Mormons," *Utah Historical Quarterly*, Winter, 1972, Vol. XL, No. 1.

Waldsmith, Thomas, "Carles Weitfle, Colorado Entrepreneur," *Stereo World*, Vol. V, No. 4, Sept.–Oct., 1978.

Watson, Elmo Scott, "Orlando Scott Goff, Pioneer Dakota Photographer," *North Dakota History*, Jan.–Apr., 1962.

———, "Photographing the Frontier," *The (Chicago) Westerners Brand Book*, Vol. IV, No. 11, Jan., 1948.

———, "Shadow Catchers of the Red Man," *(Denver) Westerners Brand Book*, Vol. VI, 1950.

Weinstein, Robert A., "Gold Rush Daguerreotypes," *The American West*, Vol. IV, No. 3, August, 1967.

Welling, William, *Photography in America: The Formative Years 1839–1900*, Thomas Y. Crowell, New York, 1978.

Wheeler, Keith, and editors, Time-Life Books, *The Townsmen*, Time-Life Books, New York, 1975.

Wittick, Tom, introduction by Terence Murphy, "An 1883 Expedition to the Grand Canyon," *The American West*, Vol. X, No. 2, Mar., 1973.

INDEX

187

188

191